FISHING
DIFFICULT WATERS
WINNING TACTICS

FISHING DIFFICULT WATERS

WINNING TACTICS

Ken Whitehead

*Foreword
by Len Cacutt*

BLANDFORD

A BLANDFORD BOOK

First published in the UK 1992
by Blandford
(a Cassell imprint)
Villiers House
41/47 Strand
London WC2N 5JE

Series editor: Jonathan Grimwood
Designer: Colin Reed
Line drawings: Ian Foulis Associates

Distributed in the United States
by Sterling Publishing Co., Inc.
387 Park Avenue South, New York, NY 10016-8810

Distributed in Australia
by Capricorn Link (Australia) Pty Ltd
P.O. Box 665, Lane Cove, NSW 2066

British Library Cataloguing in Publication Data
A catalogue record for this book is available from the British Library

ISBN 0-7137-2335-1

Typeset by Litho Link Ltd, Welshpool, Powys, Wales
Printed and bound in Great Britain by The Bath Press

CONTENTS

FOREWORD

How does one describe a happy and contented angler? Is it someone who can go to the local pond and haul out fish after fish? Is it those who take their place alongside a hundred others on a canal and catch more fish than everyone else? Is it the name at the top of this year's record for the Peruvian ginger-finned goby? Is it the designer of the latest angling gadget, or the brain behind the latest never-fail bait, the one for all seasons and species? Any one of the above may feel him- or herself to be content with one or more of these achievements. These are indeed material rewards, but they are not all there is to fishing . . .

Ken Whitehead does not judge the success of his day by the number of fish caught or the weight of one particular specimen. His day is made perfect if he has found the answer to a single fishing problem, one that would make your average angler give a Gallic shrug of the shoulders and reel in, with the comment: 'Might as well go home, the fish aren't feeding today!'

This is the point at which Ken Whitehead goes into action. He stops fishing and starts thinking. Has it happened before? Were the conditions then against feeding? For simple lack of hunger is not the answer. Unlike us, fish never know when they are hungry, their bodily functions are not under conscious control; feeding, indeed their every movement, is an automatic reaction to external or internal events.

This is not just another book on how to put maggots on a hook. The author might be described as a kind of piscatorial shrink: he has met all the problems and solved most by intuitive reasoning and close study of all things 'country'.

Importantly, the author is not simply a local expert on his own patch; he fishes all over Britain in many varied kinds of water, equally happy by a quiet pool, a tumultuous weir, a 'difficult' tidal stretch, or a river in flood.

The typical lone angler, Ken Whitehead dislikes all angling politics (not a question of left bank or right?), armchair fishers and the over-elaboration of tackle. Certainly not a recluse, he shares his answers to fishing problems through the articles and books he writes, not only on fishing but on other country pursuits. He pulls no punches, it is not his style, and I applauded his comment about non-stop fishing sessions when he said these are for 'danglers, not anglers'.

Use your brain as well as your fishing tackle, he says. In the chapter on ground-baiting, the author goes to war on the much lauded 'successful groundbait' theme so often claimed for some matchman's winning ways. Careful thought and water craft are as essential to groundbait as the ingredients in the mix, but rarely are they given enough recognition. Every chapter reveals the author's insight into particular angling problems and the answers he has arrived at.

The perfect book about fishing will never be written — after all 'fishing' is as tenuous a subject as any which does not necessarily demand an end product. One fisher's good day is another's blank, it all depends upon what the angler set out to do and what was achieved — and that does not necessarily mean lots of fish. This is Ken Whitehead's theme. Read it, digest it, then go out and practise it.

Len Cacutt

PREFACE

The angling fraternity is in great danger of outsmarting itself. We have reached a stage where anglers are convinced that the quality of fishing tackle and the amount of tackle they own will positively influence the numbers of fish they can catch. Weird and exotic baits, mounted on complicated and sometimes irresponsible rigs, are recommended as the only sure road to success; while any angler who catches specimen fish on a regular basis is portrayed as someone who practically lives on the waterside.

All of which is completely untrue. The matchman will succeed without his £1,000 of fishing tackle, and the specimen hunter will find and land big fish without spending thousands of hours fishing for them. Such success stems from water craft, the art, skill, knowledge – call it what you will – of being able to go to a swim, read the conditions of weather and water and then add to it your own experience and confidence.

In this book I have attempted to explain and expand on those qualities mentioned above. I have, I hope, pulled no punches. Any repetition or stressing in my text of styles, swims and conditions is there to reinforce an essential point.

Ken Whitehead

Chapter 1

MORNING, NOON
OR NIGHT?

If you accept the not unreasonable theory that anglers only fish when fish have got their heads down on the bottom and are feeding, then you could be forgiven for believing that they are stuffing themselves every minute of every day and night throughout the year. Why else would fishermen be sitting on the banks day in and day out, ignoring droughts, floods, ice, snow, gales and fogs, each and every one of them armed to the teeth with multiflex landing nets, bivouac umbrellas, beds, assorted laser light displays, an easy-cook stove, refrigerated food mountain, stereo transistor system, portable telephone and an early-warning bite screamer?

One school of thought is that those round-the-clock angling heroes are vigilantes who regard every next second as the precise one on which a good fish will suddenly take their bait, accepting long bouts of heavy and boring inactivity when they don't as being one of fishing's tribulations. The other hard but far more truthful school of thought, supported by a silent but knowing minority, is that the bank campers are danglers rather than anglers, fishermen who haunt the banks because they never have and probably never will stop to study and learn the feeding habits and patterns that various species of fish exhibit.

Why bother? What's so very wrong with sitting it out on the bank and waiting for it all to happen? Nothing in theory – but everything in practice. Look at it this way. Nobody will argue when I point out that complete and uninterrupted concentration is without any shadow of doubt the biggest and most effective aid to catching fish. If you don't believe that then go and watch a few well-known names performing with a rod at the next big fishing competition in your area. Despite a bank lined with supporters they will not let their attention wander for as much as a second while the competition is on.

But they don't keep that sort of effort up for days on end; four hours or so is as much as can be handled with that kind of intensity. Over and above that time concentration tends to wane and the size of the bag drops in relation to it. Now take away the match-fishing environment with its enforced time limits and substitute for it a normal fishing day. If the angler knows something of fish feeding times and patterns he could fish at those times only, accomplishing what the matchman sets out to achieve, which is maximum effort and greatest concentration combined with the best possible results. In other words he ceases being a dangler and becomes an angler.

Before we study some of the factors that influence fish feeding times let's deal with fish feeding patterns. For convenience they can loosely be split into three different types. First there is the main feeding pattern – the equivalent of our daily 'meat-and-two-veg' – which is the mainstay in providing fish energy and survival. This is the pattern we hope to find, the time when some of their natural caution is dropped and when with skill and, if necessary, some sensible groundbaiting we can catch them.

Next comes the interest feeding pattern. It has no set time and you cannot rely on it. It is the fish equivalent of our snack, when an 'interesting' item of food not strictly necessary for survival is seen and swallowed. The interest fishing pattern can often be stimulated perhaps by using an unusual bait, or by presenting an ordinary bait in an unusual style. An example would be dapping a live insect on a very hot day to catch a fish which was not showing the slightest interest in food – until it saw the hooked insect.

Finally there is the conditioned, or reactive feeding pattern. Difficult this, but it suggests a fishy reaction of 'eat first, ask questions after'. Pike which slash at a bait the second it hits the water, and salmon that are unable to feed in fresh water but which cannot resist the angler's fly or spinner are but two examples of reactive feeding.

Roach and dace which without apparent reason immediately appear from nowhere and feed when hempseeds splash on the surface of the water are further examples of conditioned feeding – but in this case conditioned by anglers repeatedly groundbaiting with loose grains. On many fisheries where the seed is in constant use nothing need be thrown into the water at all; merely the movement of the angler's arm is enough to trigger the habit.

Both the interest and conditioned or reactive feeding patterns have their place in the angler's armoury and they can be used with good effect when circumstances demand. But it is the main feeding patterns that the serious angler will want to study so that he not only recognises them, but also anticipates the times at which they are likely to occur.

There are more ideas on fish feeding times than there are restrictions on motorway driving. For years it was considered that fish fed at the crack of dawn, long before the many enemies of fish, man included, were up and about. Read all of the classic angling textbooks and you will discover that they all state categorically that unless you were in position with your float in the water as the sun actually came over the horizon you had no chance of catching a fish for the rest of the day.

But then the late-evening school of thought brought itself to notice and threw the dawn theory into the dustbin. Fish, it was claimed, not only fed equally well in the evening when falling light levels provided safety, but they offered an extra bonus to anglers by continuing to feed when the light had actually failed.

It was inevitable that the final school of thought should pour scorn on both dawn and evening feeding patterns and set out to prove that fishing through the night was the only way to get to grips with fish, especially really big specimens. As a method it came under considerable criticism from anglers of all disciplines who claimed that while there could be times when it would produce exceptional fish, it would also put fish and fisheries under pressure for 24 hours. But resistance gradually crumbled and now it is accepted and practised on many, but not all, fisheries.

So, early, late or at night, which is likely to be the best time? The easy answer to that must be all of them, because at some time or other during a 24-hour period fish of one species or another should feed. But that leads us in a circle and brings us back to the dangler, the man who sits and hopes. The easy way to answer the question is to apply a little negative thinking and work out those times when fish are not likely to feed, together with their reasons for not doing so. That at least will keep you from working your rod handle to its butt-end round the clock, fishing for no reward.

The amount of food available or the ease with which it can be taken is not the biggest influence on fish feeding times, as you could well be forgiven for imagining. It is the weather, that all-powerful element which controls the environment in which fish live. Weather affects fish through its action on the water, regulating its temperature, its oxygen content and the amount of light which it receives. All three are inter-related to some extent and each can trigger one or both of the others into action.

Let's start by studying temperature. A fish's body temperature must naturally be close to that of the water in which it is swimming. The lower that temperature the slower fish will move, the less food it will eat and the longer it will take to digest it. In other words, sport will start to slow down and eventually come to a halt. At the other extreme fish are just as susceptible to a rising temperature. The warmer the water the less the dissolved oxygen content, until there is insufficient for fish. Again they will respond by ceasing to feed.

From this it will be recognised that there must be a series of optimum temperatures between which fish will feed at their best, with extremes reducing their interest or putting them off feed altogether. Unfortunately no hard and fast rules can be laid down. There are subtle degrees of temperature variations that can happily be accepted by some species but which will be rejected by others. Generally, however, it is acknowledged that few fish feed well when the water temperature falls to 3.9°C (39°F), with interest dropping further still as the thermometer falls lower. At the other end of the scale few fish feed well when the temperature climbs to and above 21°C (70°F).

All of which proves that a thermometer should be the angler's best friend.

1. The angler's best friend. If you want to know what fish are doing, or are likely to do, the thermometer is just about the most accurate indicator.

Certainly reading the temperature when you arrive at the water (photograph 1) will give a fairly strong indication as to whether or not fish are likely to feed. But bear in mind also that it is not just violent extremes which may have taken several days to build up that influence fish feeding. Small and sudden changes – perhaps only a matter of two or three degrees within the tolerance range – can have an effect and you don't need to be on the water with a thermometer to recognise them or to anticipate when they will come.

Let's consider a couple of examples. A sharp overnight frost following several relatively warm autumn days will have provided a small temperature shift down the scale, sufficient to put fish off feed. Fish are not likely to feed again before both air and water warm – and that will probably be close to noon on the day following. There is little sense in the angler making an early start – or one at all if the hoped for temperature increase does not arrive.

At the other extreme are one or two days of frost during winter when the world becomes white and the water temperature falls sharply. The sudden arrival of a warming wind, especially a westerly, should send you scurrying for your tackle and the bankside regardless of the time, be it day or night. Get fishing, stick it out and you could be into a net full.

Blazing hot weather – and we have had some these past summers – can put fish in still waters off feed for days on end. But keep your wits about you when a weather break does arrive; small waters take less time to cool than big ones, and a sudden day of rain or even overcast skies with a cooling wind make them the sort of place to fish at any time of the day or night.

Anticipation is the name of the temperature game. Remember the weather and temperature for the past two or three days and study the forecast for what is likely to come. Once a move from a non-feeding to a feeding situation looks set to come be in a position to take advantage of it. Don't waste time on waters when it is obvious that fish are not going to feed – if you feel that you must be out and on the water choose one you are not familiar with and go and study it leaving your tackle at home. This is never time wasted.

So much for temperature and oxygen content. That light influences the feeding habits of fish is no great secret. I had a good example of it while two of us were fishing the Royalty Fishery on the River Avon in the 1990 summer of drought. It was noticeable that fish made no effort to feed through the day until the light failed as evening closed in and the sun went down.

Fish then started to feed strongly on each of the three consecutive days we were at the water. In fact we gave up fishing while the sun shone and went to the beach, making sure we were in our swims and set up by 6.30pm. That was the magic hour when rod tips started to bounce, with sport continuing until sunset and the close of the fishery.

The same has worked in reverse. While tench fishing on an Essex lake I have regularly hooked the first fish of the day as the sun actually inched over the horizon to strike the water in front of me and increase the light reaching into it. Before that – nothing. From that moment onward – everything. But so much for summertime.

Light values during winter provide a different range of feeding times. Often the weather is dull and overcast during the shortest days with the only improvement in light – if there is any at all – taking place around mid-day. Even then the increase in value may be minute with no direct sunlight hitting the water. Small though any improvement may be it will often provoke a short feeding time, better than any which may or may not occur during the early or late hours. For my money it is always the best time of day in which to concentrate, especially when pike or perch fishing.

As well as acting in the angler's favour, light values can act against him and keep fish off feed. Night after night of continuous hard frost will drop every particle of sediment and silt out of the water and leave it gin clear. As the sun rises so the temperature of the water will rise slightly – but there will be little or no sport. The reason, of course, is that bright sunlight will penetrate deep water, throwing a shadow from the finest line and making fish wary.

So the lessons to be learned from the effect that light makes to a water are self evident. Extremes at any time of year can affect sport dramatically. But an increase in light after a period of dull or overcast weather can be good news indeed regardless of the time of day or year.

Very often fish can be influenced into feeding, regardless of weather or light levels, by an alteration in the speed of the water as it flows through a fishery. Invariably such alterations are produced by human action during the warm months of the year.

An example worth describing takes place on a river close to my home where a water mill operates at a stately home during the tourist season. Each day at ten o'clock exactly the sluice is opened, the wheel starts turning and water charges down the leat, ultimately joining a small river several hundred yards below.

Once that happens, fish immediately commence feeding for a short distance downstream, continuing their interest for perhaps half or three-quarters of an hour. Then, without apparent reason, feeding stops, despite the fact that the mill is still working: that initial spurt of fresh water stirs up food and with it interest, producing fish for the net.

Other examples of man-induced water movement include pumps set along a section of marsh or fen which are operated at set times to extract water. One close to my home is used daily (other than in extreme drought) to help fill a reservoir. When this happens there is a 'draw' on the water both up and downstream of the pump, and despite the fact that it always happens at mid-day when fishing is often flat and the weather against any chance of success fish will make an immediate response by feeding.

One could go on to list many other such happenings. The paddle of a weir being drawn releasing a charge of oxygenated water and drowned insects; weed cutting which releases food among the debris as the rafts are carried downstream; the opening of a lock gate after a period of inactivity – all these are triggers that can induce feeding in a fish. Many of them take place throughout the year at exactly the same time each day. They are guaranteed feeding times and the angler should take advantage of them.

There are one or two other angling theories, not widely known, which centre again around the 'best time to fish'. They are dismissed by many without a thought, but I think that they are interesting and worth a little study. They concern the moon and its phases, tidal actions which the moon creates and the effect which those tides have on fish.

Sea fishermen are well aware that the moon governs the tide and that this in turn influences fish feeding habits. When the tide is high they will feed, and the higher the tide then very often the better chances there are of getting a good bag.

Naturally water from a rising tide will push up and along the downstream ends of a tidal river for some considerable distance. As would be expected this alteration in the water level twice a day has a considerable effect on fish that live in fresh water above the saline level, and at times of high tide they will come on feed much in the same way as those that live in the sea.

But there is a school of thought which insists that fish in waters well inland, away from the coast and completely unconnected with tidal waters, will respond to the moon and the tide in exactly the same way that sea fish do, feeding during and immediately after the time of high water.

Fact or fiction? I live close to the coast and have tried to identify this feeding influence. But my studies have not found sufficient evidence to support it in any convincing way. Yes, I have caught good fish around the time of high water when using some of the bigger inland marsh drains – but it has always been on one of those within a short distance (a mile or so) of the sea. It could well be that pressure on water tables, brought about by the rising tide, move inland to be sensed by fish which then fed much in the same manner as fish on a tideway.

Another idea connecting the moon with fish feeding times is the Solunar Theory. The folklore attached to this is that the American Indians, with their reliance on hunting and fishing, discovered that fish always reached a peak in their feeding during certain periods of the moon. They also discovered that at the other extreme there were phases of the moon when fishing and hunting were not only poor but downright impossible. Paleface settlers in the Indian territories noticed how the natives planned their hunting expeditions and quickly copied their examples – to great effect.

In the 1930s the theory came to the attention of a John Alden Knight, who set about making a detailed study of the facts. Eventually he produced the Solunar Theory and published Solunar Tables which showed the best, next best and finally the worst times of day or days in the month on which to fish. For several years they were published in American *Field Sport* magazine and proved to be very popular. I have seen a set, but I was unable to use them because unfortunately they were several years out of date. However, I studied them and it seemed to me that they were similar to the 'fishing at high tide' theory which we have already examined.

So is the Solunar Theory fact or fiction? I have had some cracking nights of sport when there has been a full moon – better by far than when the moon had been entirely absent. I have also done well on days during the new moon cycle, but not sufficiently to place reliance on it. Certainly I wouldn't entirely dismiss the idea that the moon has influence on waters away from the coast though. A full moon lifts the height of the Mississippi River by 1.8m (6ft) at its centre and on lesser waters – which must include large reservoirs and lakes in this country – by smaller amounts, and that must create a disturbance of some sort.

But despite keeping close records of the times when I have had my best – and worst – fishing days, I have yet to discover a better way of deciding when or when not to fish other than by studying the weather, light, and the water.

17

Chapter 2
TACKLING WEIRS

Like thousands of anglers across the country I'm hooked on weirs. I have only to hear the distant murmur of water as it tumbles onto the apron and roars away downstream immediately to imagine that there must be shoals of big fish just waiting to be caught in the weirpool below. But is that a fact or mere fiction? Do weirs produce more fish than other stretches of a river? Much must naturally depend on the time of year that you fish, the amount of water that is being carried and, more especially today, the structure of the weir itself.

They don't make weirs like they used to. They were once made of brick and stone with wooden boards or paddles that held the water back. Manually operated by the weir keeper, there would be at least one paddle lifted at all times to provide a constant stream.

The weir of today is likely to be plastic, working on a pressure system where volume of water forces the retaining wall under, allowing discharge to spill over the top sill across the whole of its width. These modern structures are self-adjusting according to the flow of water and need no manual regulation. For this reason alone they are fast replacing older models which require major maintenance and expensive repairs.

From the angler's point of view the difference between the two systems centres on the amount of current they supply and on the way that they provided it. In theory fishing should be the same below either type, but in practice there will be a better response below the older, solid structure, where a concentrated outfall of water escapes, than from the new plastic barriers which supply a wide, slow trickle with little if any effect on water in the pool below or farther downstream.

When weirs are successful it is because of the fast-moving water they create. This supplies fish with two vital and live-giving ingredients, oxygen and food, when they need it most. As far as oxygen is concerned the demand is greatest during warm summer and autumn months when levels are low along the main river. Then, fish of all species will move into the weirpool, even those that normally prefer slow or near-static water such as bream, tench and carp.

Food may be provided in two ways, either through items being washed downstream and over the weir or disturbed from the banks and the river bed itself by the action of the water as it works through and around the pool. It is a year-round happening that holds many fish permanently in the vicinity of the

2. One of the old types of weir where current is constant (see far bank) and so are the snags. But fishing throughout the year remains good, regardless of the weather.

weir and even far below it, something that the thinking angler is well aware of and prepared to use to his advantage.

Beware of rushing into weir fishing without first studying and then remembering its pros and cons. Enthusiasm helps catch a fish, but confidence catches a bigger one. In favour of weir fishing is the fact that fast-running water will help to make the angler less conspicuous from his position on the bank – providing that he blends with the background and does not stand above the skyline. And because of the varying water depths, the large area of the pool, the strength and variety of currents, as well as the many different species of fish which may be present, there will be a chance to ring the changes throughout the day and use a wide variety of rigs and tactics, one of which should bring success.

But there are plenty of problems on the debit side, not the least being that fishing a weir is very hard work. First you must decide where the fish are likely to be, and there are no hard and fast rules to help you make that decision. Of

3. Silkweed; that below is fine and easily fastened to the hook. Shown above is water moss, unattractive to fish and impossible to fasten to the hook.

course, much will depend on the species; for example, barbel often move up the pool until they are practically under the lip of the apron while the weather remains warm. Once it cools then they will drop back into the deep water that has been scoured out by the current. But when will they move? Where exactly will they lie in relation to the race itself?

Then there is the question of physical effort. Once the angler decides to fish a pool he will be faced with a day of constant casting and re-casting regardless of whether he legers or decides to swim the stream. This means planning well in advance and selecting the right tackle for the job. A tried and tested well-balanced rod, a reel with high-ratio pick-up and suitable line make the difference between heaven and hell after four hours of intense fishing. It is more than likely that during the day terminal tackle will be lost (often quantities of it) and that means carrying spares, especially swim feeders, leads and stops. Which is a timely reminder that nothing succeeds without planning.

Don't expect to drop into a good clean swim around a weirpool every time that you make a visit – not even the one that you fished with such success during the previous week. Throughout the year debris of every description is washed downstream either over or through the weir itself and eventually into the pool where it will collect, often becoming silted into place to become a permanent feature. This picture changes constantly with each sudden flood or spurt of water during summer as well as winter, altering the shape of the bed, the depth of swims, and where the rubbish is stacked and held.

There is only one way to get to know and understand the basic topography and major snags of a weir. With the commencement of each season study the pool through polarising glasses and then plumb, sound and drag the bottom with a leger lead attached to the end of your line (without a hook) and keep at it until all obstructed and other no-go areas are found and their extent known. At the same time you will be able to form a picture of where deeper water lies, and compare it with those same places of last year. If you cannot remember them all (something not impossible on some of the large lower pools on our big rivers) commit your findings to a chart. Laborious as the task may be, it will help build up an extremely useful record and allow you to make some interesting comparisons after a few seasons have passed.

There is a bewildering range of baits available for weir fishing all of which can catch fish at some time. Many of them are bizarre and only provide results at a particular time in the season or in one particular part of the pool, remaining without interest or success when fished at other times and places. Cherries, cubes of banana and snowberries freelined in slack water or cast under the lip of the apron are but a few that have been tried and proved.

But in its season there is one special bait that will take practically every fish to be found in a weirpool with the possible exception of predators such as pike or eels. It costs nothing, does not need packing or carrying and is never in short supply. That bait is silkweed, the fine, near-slime type of green weed adhering to every brick, wooden support, concrete ledge and post at and below the water level. (See photograph 3) Fish do not need to search for it before they can feed – a constant supply is always available as it is pushed and dragged from where it grows by the force of water.

Silkweed fishing has a style and a skill of its own. It is unusual in that it requires both sight and touch combined to detect a bite, but apart from that needs no special tackle. Any rod that is 3.6m (12ft) or more in length together with a free running reel loaded with line around the 1.3kg (3lb) breaking strain mark will suffice. But some thought must be put into selecting a float.

It is essential to have a float that can easily be seen and yet capable of allowing the line between float and rod tip to be kept tight. That means something bigger than the normal, but definitely not big and clumsy. One of the Avon varieties will do, its size depending on the flow. Better still is a float that is thicker in circumference on the water line. In a tackle shop I managed to find a supply of short, round floats that used to be described as perch bobbers and these are ideal for the job. Should the float be submerged by rough water then the distinct hard 'knock' given by a fish taking the bait will still be felt along the length of the tightened line. An immediate strike drives the hooks home. Notice that I wrote *hooks*. It is possible to use a single, but a very small treble (size 12 or under) is a better proposition, not merely to increase hooking power but to support the bait correctly.

One of the main reasons that fish accept silkweed is because it is full of minute insect and crustacean life. Squeeze it or crush it in any way and you immediately reduce its attraction and food value – so the less it is handled the better. The easy way of collecting weed intended for hookbait is to use the handle of a landing net and rub it free from the supports on which it is growing, then lift it without crushing into a deep bait box filled with water, tucking it away in the shade until it is wanted.

To bait the hook just drag the treble through the box several times and then twist it around until the weed has tangled into a ball. With the float adjusted so that the bait will swim between 0.6–0.9m (2–3ft) below the surface a surprising number of casts can be made before it will work loose and need replacing.

If you are able to get down and fish from the sill of the weir then so much the better. All you need do is to let the baited hook drop in the water beside the race, close to your feet, and allow it to run downstream paying line out so that it is carried away unhindered. It will increase your chances if you groundbait a little. All you need do is to scuff your wader on the sill itself, releasing a dark cloud of particles and weed that will sweep downstream around your bait. That will be more than enough to attract fish.

There is a definite season for silkweeding. During the early months when weed is sprouting and a bright, near pea green in colour it will be readily accepted by roach and dace. At that time the bites are always razor sharp, just like those you get when hempseed fishing.

As the season progresses the growth rates will increase, and the colour of the weed darken. It also seems that the darker the weed becomes the better fish like it so that by autumn you will find good roach, dace and chub almost wallowing as they leisurely suck the baited hook into their mouths.

Fishing the live minnow is another angling method largely practised in weirpools. It closely follows silkweeding in style, tackle and tactics. Cannibalism is a fact of life around any weir. Many species, even those normally imagined as weed and insect eaters, will take to snapping up small fry, minnows especially, in the early part of the season. It is a knock-on from spawning time when both eggs and newly hatched fry are accepted by mature fish as being part of the food cycle.

Minnows, together with the fry of roach, dace, or any of the silver-scaled fish up to 7.6cm (3in) or so in length, make the most successful baits, hooked through the top lip only and fished without the encumbrance of wire traces and numerous swivels. Catch them with a very small float-fished hook and bait, or use a drop net in the shallows, perhaps a collapsed keepnet lying on the bottom with a string leading from its rim. Baited with a small piece of crust it is a simple matter to lift it onto the bank when sufficient fish are feeding over it, trapping them inside.

Keep the breaking strain of the line low, 2.2–2.7kg (5–6lb) at the most, and choose a float that will carry several AA or bigger lead substitute shot. These should be attached well down the line, helping to keep the bait below the surface. Again float visibility is all important, so make sure that you select one which has a fairly large circumference and be prepared to ring the changes with colours as light values alter during the day.

This is another task for a long rod. Drop the baited hook at your feet then let it work downstream beside the race, holding it back once it gets close to the tail of the pool. By checking line or moving the rod tip either to left or right the float can be made to hold and follow in that same direction, working into slack water or across the rapids, covering wide expanses of water without great effort on the part of the angler.

Problems of control increase where it is not possible to get onto the sill of the weir. It means the angler must fish from a bank, and that demands constant re-casting to keep the bait out into the stream. When this situation is forced upon you or when the area to be covered is heavy with underwater obstruction I prefer to use the paternoster. There are two methods of making a break-free paternoster rig suitable for weirpools, especially those that are full of snags. One is to secure a small swivel to the line, followed by a length of low breaking strain monofiliment fastened to the opposite eye of the swivel. A lead should be secured at the terminal end of the weaker mono just large enough to hold the bottom.

From the upper eye of the swivel a monofiliment link 0.6m (2ft) or so in length can be attached, finishing at the hook and bait. If snagged, a strong pull will snap the weak line, ditching the lead and freeing the rig completely. The alternative, suitable only when there is no strong current, is to use several very large shot pinched to the terminal end of the line in place of a solid weight. When snagged these leads soon pull free, releasing line and bait.

Working the bait is easy. Cast upstream to the edge of the race and as close under the sill as possible, then 'bounce' weight and bait downstream by holding back the rod tip, letting the current take the rig, then lowering the tip after letting out a little line. As the lead hits bottom again wait a minute or so, then repeat the exercise. When the bait has reached the end of the run work it back to your feet by using the sink-and-draw method. Remember that bites can only be felt, so it is essential to keep the line between rod tip and lead as tight as possible. When a fish takes strike immediately, don't wait.

There is a welcome shift away from livebaiting today in favour of deadbaits. Dead minnows are just as attractive – and deadly – as the live fish. In fact there is little to choose in their action through rough water, both turning and twisting as they work downstream. That is the secret of fishing the minnow – keeping it on the move. Once offered in still water they loose a great deal of their 'grab and run' attraction.

Old-time anglers who fished the Thames weirs for trout would mount two small trebles one above the other, and on each hook mount a minnow. Fished with a float the effect was that of a small shoal moving together through the water. They described it as 'killing'. It bears some thought and possible experiment.

It is not possible to talk of weirs without considering fishing for barbel. Their natural home for much of the year, barbel are seldom taken from the pools in great numbers other than during the warm months, and then only by anglers who study where they are and how best to reach them. Chuck-and-chance tactics will usually prove to be a complete waste of time.

Barbel have an uncanny knack of finding a small area of calm, current-free water in the centre of mass disturbance. It may be a ledge, rock or similar obstruction set in the bottom that provides shelter, or a trough of deeper water formed by a channel in the bed of the river in which they can lie using the minimum amount of energy. Few such places are without a barbel during the season, none of them is ever easy to cast to, and all can take a heavy toll in tackle.

Only one tactic will put the angler in with a fighting chance and that is to bring the fish out into the open water, away from obstructions, and with an interest in feeding, which means using some pretty potent groundbait that must be very accurately placed.

Everybody is familiar with the groundbaiting tactics adopted in Edwardian times, when lobworms were dug in their thousands and fed into a selected swim for days on end before anglers took up their fishing stations. Today it would be an excessively expensive undertaking both in time and money. But there are substitutes for the worm mountains once considered necessary. Two of the most successful, which complement each other, are meat and blood.

Blood can be obtained from an abattoir, a pint or so being sufficient for a day's fishing. When combined with bread, bran, crushed potato or other similar heavy base feed it will act as a binding agent and release a scent trail that will quickly spread downstream. But getting groundbait into the exact position where it will influence barbel and, more important still, getting it quickly to the bottom can be desperately difficult. If the current is not too strong then large balls weighted with stones will suffice. Mixing a quantity of earth with groundbait in the bucket can also give extra weight.

Where these tactics fail or the area is unsuitable for their use then one must use the swimfeeder, open ended and as large as possible. With the help of some accurate casting it will lay a trail of groundbait and after a time saturate the area. It is a slow business and there will certainly be a great deal of tackle lost. All the angler can do is to grin and bear it knowing that the ends will justify the means.

Meat hookbaits that complement blood groundbait include luncheon meat, corned beef, sausages both cooked and raw, sausage meat stiffened with bread, raw liver and pork loaf. During the heat of summer they must be kept cool if they are to remain firm and stay on the hook, and it is worth the hassle of carrying them in an ice box. Don't be frightened to use hefty sized cubes where the water is fast flowing, or to use blotting paper pads behind the barb of the hook to wedge the softer offerings in place.

The speed of a barbel bite must be seen to be believed. Many anglers set their rod in a rest and watch the rod tip, hoping that they can pick it up quickly enough to drive home the hook while a fish still has it in its mouth and before the bait is dropped. Many set their faith in hoping that the bite will be so firm and decisive that the fish will hook itself. Both methods are a prizeless gamble.

The barbel expert will sit holding the rod-butt in his hands with the top joint supported in a rest at all times, feeling the line and ready to make a firm upward sweep with the tip the moment that interest is felt. On the River Lee I once watched an angler, using this method at King Weir, hook five barbel out of six bites. The fish were lying under the lip of the apron, surrounded by snags and obstructions, and only that immediate strike and some hefty side strain could drag them out into the open and subsequently into the landing net.

Chapter 3

IN TIMES OF FLOOD

Everybody talks about floodwater, but hardly anyone bothers to fish when floods are up and running. If you dispute this, take a look along the banks next time the waters rise and make a note of the vacant swims. Better still, examine those swims that are occupied and then analyse why anglers are fishing them.

Finally, decide for yourself whether you would have chosen one of them, or whether with your knowledge of the water you would have settled elsewhere. If you can do that with some certainty then you are well on the way to becoming a flood man, and should be out there doing it and not just watching.

The vast majority of anglers avoid fishing in floodwater because they dislike the physical effort of having to make repeated casts in order to keep a bait in the swim; of becoming snagged at regular intervals either on the bottom or on water-borne rubbish; of breaks and lost gear or, worst of all, losing a good fish because floodwater has got behind it and carried it downstream.

How much is fact and how much just old-fashioned fiction? Well, if you insist on fishing your favourite swim expecting it to be its normal obliging self, or you set out to find a swim where you are going to sit in comfort and shelter without giving a thought about the water and where or what fish will be doing – hard luck! Yes, you will lose some tackle, need repeatedly to recast your bait, and under Section One of Sods Law lose one or two fish. But with imagination and care losses of all sorts can be kept to a minimum.

Start by appreciating that to fish on the top of the flood, when water is at its highest and the river has become a raging torrent, is a mug's game. I've tried it umpteen times and the odd fish that I have managed to catch have never been worth the effort, nor wear and tear on tackle that went into their taking. The time to fish floodwater is 24 hours or so after it has reached its peak, when some of the steam is going out of the stream and, more important still, when the colour is fining down and the water has ceased to look like a sample drawn from a bottle of Guinness.

Once fish are able to see or to sense a bait then you must put yourself in their

OPPOSITE
4. Searching slack water downstream of the angler, close to the opposite bank.

place and mentally work out positions where you would go to find protection away from the main thrust of the current, and where food could be found without the energy-consuming effort of hard searching. If you tackle that job properly then it's an even bet that the list of places you select will all have one thing in common. They will feature obstructions, either natural or man made, set against the banks.

Here is a check list of places which I have successfully fished or where I have seen good fish taken at floodtime, together with my reasons for their selection.

Slack water Books describe it and anglers acknowledge its existence but few really know what slack water looks like at flood time. It is not an area of water where there is no movement of any sort. That is dead water – and dead water in times of flood will be thick with suspended mud and silt, not the sort of place that fish will want to inhabit. Slack water has movement without any of the rush and force of floodwater and will frequently be found on bends, where the flow pushing against the concave bank leaves slow (slack) water on the downstream side of the convex bank opposite. Photograph 4 illustrates this.

Depressions Not connected with anglers unsuccessfully fishing floods – but level areas of the river bed in which there is a sudden deep hole or long gully. They are important because fast water will pass over them completely, forming a sheltered space within the depression that will often hold a good head of fish for the duration of the spate. Providing that they are not out of casting distance from the bank depressions can bring a high success rate.

Side entrances Streams, brooks, drains – even land drains draining fields – will provide areas where the main current is diverted and broken. But beware: often those feeders carry an enormous amount of silt and debris along with them, making them unpopular with fish. Let the current bring clearer water before you tackle them.

Cowdrinks An angling term used to describe sections of the bankside where cattle regularly drink throughout the year. Many such places are not worthy of the name. A cattle drink suitable for fishing in floodwater is one where the banks are trodden down and eroded for some distance inland, making an area away from the main current which fish can use once it is covered. Photograph 5 shows one that produced good roach and chub at flood time.

Eddies Water pushing downstream past a break in the bank will provide a small area where water circulates quietly, often in a reverse direction of the main current. Even the smallest is worth investigating.

Rubbish rafts Held in place by slack water, often in eddies, this accumulated natural and human debris will provide both shelter and food for fish.

Islands The downstream ends are always good, and often provide a place where it will be possible to swim the stream with suitable float tackle.

Moorings, marinas and boat yards Berths, moored boats and slipways all provide a slowing down of water and shelter that can be used to advantage. Often

*5. A good, old-fashioned cattle drink where fish seek shelter
when flood water is running.*

they also provide rubbish rafts. Strangely, once the water recedes again they won't be anywhere near as prolific.

Bridges On the downstream side there will be eddies which will hold fish – and in many cases a fair amount of trapped rubbish as well. If you don't want to lose a lot of tackle investigate them thoroughly before committing yourself for the day.

Locks Out of use to traffic for the duration of a flood, the downstream end of a lock cutting provides ideal water where near-normal fishing can take place. They are not always packed solidly with fish as one would expect, but I have often had good bags of eels when flood-dodging below locks – especially during the winter months.

Underwater obstructions Not those sudden heaps of logs, plastic bags and dead sheep that appear with the flood, but obstructions that have been in place for years and are heavily silted or fixed to the bed so as to become part of the regular features of the fishery. Fallen trees, the foundations of an old footbridge or boathouse that has rotted away, cable conduits and large water or drainage pipes laid across the river bed are all places where fish will head for and use for

29

shelter during floods. Normally you would fight shy of them because of the risk of losing tackle. But when the water rises they hold good fish, and you should be prepared to take a risk.

Those are just a few ideas as to where you should look – but avoid the trap of being dogmatic and forcing yourself to stay in one place because fish should be there. You need to keep the tackle mountain to a minimum, and your get-up-and-go options well to the front. No easy thing when you consider that heavy and continued rain demands full waterproof clothing, that the banks will probably be a mass of thick, clinging mud – and that the path from one section of river to another may be nearly impassable.

So far we have only considered getting out of the main current in our theoretical search for fish. But there will be plenty of them still out where it runs fast – even in mid-stream. And there is an even chance of getting to grips with them providing your tackle matches the challenge with which you are faced.

Keep in mind that whether there is a flood or not running water is always faster on the surface and a great deal slower close to the river bed. You are going to need enough weight to take a bait to the bottom and then hold it in place which means that rod, reel and line should all be in perfect balance. If you can achieve that, then you will find it still delicate enough to record bites and sensitively handle a hooked fish. Tackle straight from your sea-fishing gear just won't do.

I favour the paternoster rig for main-stream fishing, selecting a lead which I consider will be just, and only just heavy enough to hold bottom, tied to a break-free length of nylon finer than my reel line with the aid of a three-way swivel. It is possible to get these in small sizes, coloured black. They won't show and won't allow line to tangle, providing you keep the hook link as long as the distance between swivel and end lead only. Lengths of hook link beyond that merely tangle and disguise bites. By switching to a lighter weight the current will carry both it and the bait bumping away downstream and this can search out fairly long stretches where the bed is known to be clear.

For legering close to the bank there is nothing to beat the link leger, using a low breaking-strain link between split ring and lead. The beauty of the link leger is that should it tangle, then the lead will break free allowing the hook to ride clear.

Whether you choose to set up a swing or quivertip tip section to indicate bites is a matter of choice. I find that floodwater fish tend to hit the bait good and hard, possibly because they 'know' that if it is not grabbed it will be swept away. For this reason alone I often dispense with both aids and watch the rod tip itself. Stiff though it may be in comparison with the swing or quiver, it often bounces a good 15cm (6in) or more when it registers a bite. There have also been occasions when I have had the rod jerked out of its rests, so it pays to keep the handle close to hand.

Where it is possible to float fish, use an Avon-type float with a clear, plastic body cocked by means of a swan shot link weight. If there is slightly more

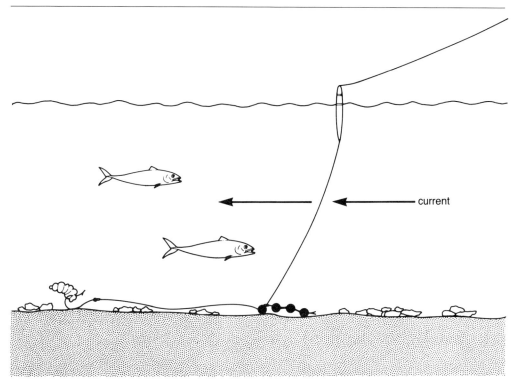

Diagram 1. *Laying-on using a swan shot link for weight.*

distance between float and link than there is depth then laying-on as well as swimming the stream can be practised, holding the float back and allowing the link to rest on the bed. Again, should the leads catch it will be possible to free the line, losing a few shot without suffering a break. (See diagram 1)

How to groundbait? If you are using the paternoster in heavy water then a block-end feeder attached with the lead is about your only chance of spreading the gospel. On the rare occasions when I know the bottom to be reasonably clear I use one, loading it with a stiff bread and bran or crushed potato mixture plus a few white maggots. The light colour will attract fish. Other than that, groundbaiting in really heavy water can be a chuck-and-chance-it game.

Close to the banks, then normal bread and bran balls weighted with a stone to make them sink is a sensible choice, thrown well upstream of the swim. Better still are brown paper bags half filled with bait together with a really heavy weight, tied at the neck. They won't guarantee landing in the correct place – measuring drift is anyone's guess in fast-moving water – but they will ensure that the bait lands pretty much in one place and together before it is spread around.

When link legering I use mashed bread which is stiffened with some clay or sausage rusk as groundbait, squeezing a fair-sized ball of this on to the lead.

31

Properly mixed it will sink like the proverbial stone, either breaking free on striking, or working loose with the action of the water. Either way, you can feel through the line and rod when the parting of the way occurs.

Finally, if it is possible to use float tackle then it should be possible to groundbait with the aid of a bait layer, even though it may mean arming the lead already fitted to it with extra weight in the form of lead wire in an effort to make the layer, which will tend to kite in fast water and sink quickly and efficiently. If you really want to do things on a grand scale, there is the Rubby Dubby tin, an extension of the bait layer described in Chapter 11 on Baiting and Raking.

By tradition the lobworm is accepted as the only hookbait worth using in floods. In theory it's a grand idea which conjures up vision of lobworms in their thousands being drowned, washed off the land and into the river, inciting fish to a frenzy of feeding. In practice the numbers of lobworms that you actually see dead on the banks wouldn't fill a ferret's handbag.

By all means use the worm, but don't expect it to perform miracles. Remember that the water itself is dark with suspended silt and that a dark worm isn't doing a great deal to advertise itself either by colour or scent.

Big is beautiful under flood conditions and if the bait is light in colour or is likely to give off a fair amount of scent then so much the better. I've had success with moulded cheese and bread paste, large pieces of cheese cut into irregular shapes that will turn and move with the current, pieces of sausage meat stiffened with rusk, and big cubes of luncheon meat. Think in terms of golf ball sizes, use hooks in keeping and you will be along the right lines.

Of course floodwater will affect still waters as well as rivers and streams, especially small ponds and lakes. Here it is not so much the height of the water that is the problem, but the colour it will take even after a little rain.

Though fish will not be so hard to reach as those that live in rivers they can still be difficult to bring on feed. Getting them started is the greatest problem, and the only successful trick I know is to use the finest and lightest-coloured groundbait you can get your hands on. I plump for white breadcrumbs, and even go to the trouble to dry and crush my own so that yellow colouring from the crust is not included. Unlike their river counterparts still-water fish at floodtime do not need the enormous increase in hook bait and hook sizes; keep them small and ring the bait changes.

Whatever you do, and however you do it, don't give up trying or concentrating when you are fishing flood water. If baits, groundbaits, rigs, prayers and bad language are of no avail, but your instinct and analyses of the water tell you that the swim is right, step up the concentration. More than one specimen fish has abandoned an inbuilt caution and finished up in the net when all was thought to be lost.

Chapter 4
SMALL IS BEAUTIFUL

It is a hard and chilling fact that 70 per cent of all ponds in Britain have been lost since the start of the century. Many of them were built with a special purpose in mind but are now no longer needed and have fallen into disuse. A good example are the Sussex hammer ponds built during the Industrial Revolution to provide power for forge hammers. Other ponds were built to provide power for water wheels, or were dug out for clay, used to make bricks for house building. But the majority were dug and designed as cattle drinks, which is probably their greatest use today.

Their loss has been hastened through in-filling by developers so that land is available for building, or from the so-called 'Nanny Syndrome', the product of pressure from the community to fill and level any piece of water into which people may possibly fall. But the final blow to ponds — even some of the well-known ones — has been the drought conditions that have prevailed during the past few seasons. Many waters dried out, exposing the bed which then cracked and split through the effect of prolonged heat. When rains finally came they were no longer watertight and joined the legion of the lost.

The passing of so many small waters has done a great deal to decimate much of our wild life, especially aquatic insects and vertebrates, and to cause the collapse of numerous well-established and productive fisheries. Those left are suffering increased fishing pressure and this, combined with continuing low water tables, is producing an unprecedented challenge to anglers and angling.

For pond enthusiasts who are looking for new waters or those who want a fishery of their own there is no time to lose in starting a search. Ignore the large scale Ordnance Survey maps so often recommended; a large percentage of waters that they show will have dried out. Instead take to the roads and footpaths during autumn and winter when leaves are off the trees, allowing waters hidden during the summer to be seen. It is amazing what turns up; I found two new ponds last winter still being used as cattle drinks each of which held fish, neither more than 9m (10 yards) from a road along which I have travelled every day for the past five years.

What is a pond? In my definition it is any piece of water where you can cast into the centre using a reasonable float rig. 'Reasonable' in this instance describes floats, hooks and weights that would not scare fish as they landed on the surface.

Waters bigger than those come under the heading of lakes and need a different approach altogether.

What is a good pond likely to hold in the way of fish, or, more important, be able to support once it has been stocked? Everything depends on the location of the water and the surroundings. Farming and agricultural progress rate rank high on the debit side. Ponds set low down below sloping fields or in a valley are quite capable of being polluted out of existence if field fertilisers drain and seep into them. Even if the pollutant does not kill fish, in all probability it will stimulate weed growth which will stifle and eventually choke the water.

Trees are probably the worst enemies of ponds, over the years their leaves settling on to the bottom to rot and provide a thick carpet of silt that will encourage gas discharge, lower the oxygen level, kill weed and reduce the water depth until it dries out completely.

Good waters have a balance of surrounding trees and bushes providing cover, shelter and protection from wind and sun, plus an area of deep water combined with weeded shallows. Those that I know are not in that condition through chance — they have been managed either by the owner or by a club.

The size of the pond need not bear relation to the different species it may contain, or their weight. Mostly you will catch carp both common or wild, mirror, leather and crucian plus tench, rudd, roach, perch, pike and eels. I have yet to fish a pond that has held a head of good (as opposed to a good head of) roach and perch — and the same goes for bream which in my part of the country are almost entirely absent. Few ponds are without a population of hybrid fish, mostly rudd × roach but often including carp crosses that can be difficult to tell from the pure bred specimen.

Never think that small ponds don't, or can't, hold big fish. I have caught or seen lying on the bank carp up to 5.4kg (12lb), crucian carp to 1.3kg (3lb), tench to 2kg (4½lb) and rudd to 0.9kg (2lb). Some of the eels that I've caught or weighed have scaled 1.5–1.8kg (3½–4lb) and I have seen bigger and better caught by anglers who have been loath to handle and weigh them! Hardly a week will pass without the angling press featuring bigger and better specimens taken from a small pond, some often close to record figures.

Whether you will catch fish in that category must naturally depend on their being in the water! The trouble (or should it be the fascination?) is that few anglers or angling clubs really know what the pond in front of them contains. Word of mouth usually amounts to rumour which is no ground on which to build fish facts. So whether you are new to the water or have fished it for years always plan and tackle it as if you expect to catch the fish of a lifetime. There is rarely any proof that it won't be there.

The first and most important skill in pond fishing is water craft. Without it you will never really succeed. To practise it requires thought, planning and a fair amount of self-control. It is as well to start by getting some sizes in perspective, commencing with an angler 1.8m (6ft) tall walking towards the water's edge. Irrespective of the vibrations he creates, his height alone will ensure that he will be seen by fish in a small water well before he reaches the swim he want to fish from.

If he wants to have a walk around before deciding which is the best swim to settle in then you can bet that practically every fish in the pond will have been alerted before he has finished.

Now add to the scene a long rod – perhaps a roachpole – which is put together and waved over the water every time that a cast is made. Even 4.5m (15ft) of rod held vertically by an angler standing up will bring its tip at least 5.4m (18ft) above the bank, ensuring that it or its movements will be seen by fish right out to the centre of the pond.

Good water craft starts with camouflaged clothing to reduce the angler's visibility by blending him into the background. It includes putting the rods together long before the swim is reached and, using cover, a careful stalk to the edge of the bank. It is worth cultivating the old dodge of 'talking' birds off the water, holding a make-believe conversation loud enough to ensure that they hear and slip quietly away instead of suddenly blasting off in an explosion of wings.

Then, and only then should the water be examined with the aid of polarising glasses and, if it is the first visit, possibly a pair of binoculars to establish areas which might hold fish. Likely signs are surface bubbles or mud-clouded water, both of which are produced by fish feeding on the bottom. Movement of weed and reeds produced by fish pushing through them as they search for food or shelter is another. Occasionally fish will be seen basking near to the surface either as individuals or in a shoal; it is worth remembering that fish in that position are not only difficult to catch, but also pick up the smallest movement or vibration. If they are put down most other fish will follow suit.

Whether or not you are the first or are likely to be the only person fishing the pond must govern the actual swim you occupy and the tactics you should use. If other anglers are present then count on fish having already been disturbed and that they will have moved towards the centre. Nothing further can be lost, so settle at the water's edge and cast well out to get among them. If you are alone then there is little sense in wasting time by making long casts. You will probably be casting over fish, quite happily feeding around the margins.

Groundbaits and groundbaiting can be a vexed question where such small areas of water are concerned. Heavy groundbaiting – and I include pre-baiting a water in this category – will occasionally work. But during long, dry periods of summer when the water level is low it can often prove to be counter-productive. The risk comes from fish that might not be in the mood to feed, leaving areas of bait untouched to ferment and help further reduce the oxygen content in the water. But that is not the only risk.

Large areas of fine groundbait will often attract and hold large numbers of

small fish literally crowding out bigger and better specimens. Once there they are difficult to move – and adding more groundbait will do nothing to improve the situation. Yes, there are times when baiting up pays with either the standard bread and bran mix or a good cloud bait but think before you pitch it in with abandon.

In particular don't over apply it if the water is clear, because the light-coloured areas on the bottom will stand out like a beacon. Far better to use loose pieces of your hook offering cast around a tight, small area in the swim which will provide just the right amount of interest. This especially applies during the cold winter months.

There are three areas where fish can be found feeding in a pond – on the surface, in mid-water and on the bottom. There are four sound, tried and tested rigs that will show them a bait and allow the angler to come to terms with them while they are in those positions. They include surface floated baits, baits fished on the drop, baits fished by the lift method, and freelining. Which method you select must be governed by water and weather conditions.

First, surface fishing. Large pieces of bread crust, boilies, grasshoppers and other natural 'floaters' freelined without a float and weight but perhaps with some assistance from a small bubble float are all good. They don't need to be cast to the middle of the pond – in fact they will do best close to margin weed. Occasional offerings of small pieces of floating crust are sometimes used as groundbait, but they usually attract the smaller fish.

Fishing on the drop is excellent for mid-water feeders – rudd and roach especially. The rig is simple. A self-cocking or similar small float is mounted and weight added either on to the float or to the line immediately below it so that both hook and bait will sink slowly under their own weight. If fish are exceptionally float-shy, try using a small piece of bottle cork weighted in the same way. Successful hook baits include maggot, paste or sweetcorn and a few pieces of these can be used loosely cast around the float as groundbait.

The lift method of fishing is deadly. Fasten a small piece of peacock quill or a small stick float by one end only, and fix one AAA lead substitute shot 15cm (6in) above the hook. Set the distance between shot and float slightly above the actual depth, and after casting tighten line so that the float sinks and is held down till just the tip shows.

Once a fish takes the bait the weight will be lifted, the float will lie flat and a gentle strike will hook the fish. Be sensible when groundbaiting; don't spread so much on the bottom that the hook is swamped and remains unseen. Remember

OPPOSITE
6. Where other anglers are on a small water fish will tend to move into the centre. The roachpole is an ideal rod for this situation – but un-ship joints rather than wave the whole rod vertically over the surface.

also to use the lift method after an hour or so of fishing on the drop. It will guarantee that you connect with bigger fish that have been feeding on the bottom taking loose offerings which have filtered past smaller fish in mid-water.

Finally, legering. Use any bait you like, fasten either a lead substitute swan shot leger or just two or three AAA lead substitute shot pinched directly to the line a short distance above the hook, and then squeeze a small ball of stiff groundbait around the lead. This weight will allow a gentle cast to take the bait where it is wanted with the groundbait soaking and falling away once it hits the bottom.

Keep everything small and fine, avoid casting long distances, don't be frightened to fish over and into weedbeds and you will be well on the way to success. If there is a wind blowing across the water try freelining close to the bank against which it is being driven. The water temperature against that shore will be slightly warmer than on the one opposite and the drift will carry food with it. Not only that, but the ripple will hide glint from your line during bright sunshine.

One final fish not mentioned so far is the pike. Small ponds can hold big pike — and that is no old wives' tale. One little pond not two miles from my home once produced a fish of 8kg (18lb) which frightened the life out of the angler whose lobworm it took. It also caused a two-deep queue around the banks for the following six months as anglers tried to catch the fish again.

Moral? If you know a pond holds big fish of any species keep your mouth closed. If the big fish are pike then normally they reach the net of an angler who is deadbaiting for eels. But deadbaiting is not the only successful method. Try working a sprat sink-and-draw across the water, or use a shallow-diving plug. Providing the water is not whipped into a frenzy there will be little chance of putting a pike down.

Disturbance is hard to avoid when a fish of any species is being played. Side strain is important, to prevent it being pulled to the surface where it will flap and splash, but more so is remembering to keep seated not only when playing, but when actually landing a fish. Shadow, especially one from a human, will frighten off every other fish in the water.

Chapter 5

BREAKING THE DROUGHT

There will never be a better time to stop and study both tackle and tactics than during the period of a long, hard drought. For the past few seasons anglers have been battling with their fair share of hot weather and there is every reason to believe that more is to come. What many anglers have avoided is reaching any concrete conclusions on just how to deal with fish during sky-high summer temperatures.

Fishing problems for the angler start and finish with the sun. It provides a formula that runs along the lines of:

> sun = heat = drought
> ∴ drought = evaporated water = low water levels
> ∴ low water levels = reduced oxygen levels
> ∴ low levels + increased heat = increased weed growth
> ∴ increased weed = further reduced water levels

And by carrying on you will eventually reach a point where both water and fish levels on small lakes and ponds become damaged beyond repair as the drought lengthens. Small wonder that drought malaise, a loss of interest in fish, fishing or anything connected with the subject strikes down even the most enterprising angler at such times.

The best way to tackle drought is to study and then implement the *When, Where and How* formula. Quite simply, it means preparing a plan to deal separately with each water that you intend to fish, completely abandoning the usual approach in favour of one to suit the mood of the fish and the state of the fishery. It can best be summed up by the angler being prepared to get mobile and search for fish rather than sitting on a tackle box and waiting for the fish to come to him.

Make a start by studying *When*. Not surprisingly most anglers plump for the early and late fishing hours. After all, they have always been chosen by the vast majority as the only times when fish will feed during summer months and for several well-considered reasons. It makes sense that with no sun on the water, the water temperature must be lower, making fish more active. There will also be less light actually shining through the water, less chance for the angler to be seen, and less disturbance to fish life from the public and associated activities which take place on or close to the banks. That includes passing boats, swimmers, and dog walkers and there are others . . .

Unfortunately fish will refuse to play by the normal rules of fishing during a long drought. Temperature is the main reason; the higher the water temperature rises then the less interest they will show in feeding whatever the time of day. And as they can and often do go for long periods without needing to feed at all it can only be the angler who eventually suffers regardless of how long he may sit it out, or how early or late he fishes.

But there are feeding patterns other than the main one of the day as we discussed and discovered in Chapter 1. The interest pattern, where either a bait or the way it is presented is used to arouse attention from seemingly uninterested fish should now be the priority and it can be created at any time during the 24 hours – but only when the angler has completely disposed of all his preconceived ideas on set fishing times.

Having settled *When* to fish we must next study *Where.* That can be fairly easily defined as out of direct sunlight and in places where the water is cool and holding a high oxygen content. Of course fish do lie in direct sunlight, but basking fish are rarely feeding fish, and it is fish that might feed which we are interested in, and that we intend to interest.

Let's study a few such places starting with those that are cool. On still-water fisheries, water is at its heaviest at a temperature of 4°C (39.2°F). This means that whenever the temperature on the surface is below that mark the deepest water will be the warmest. And far more to the point for the purpose of this chapter is the fact that when the surface water is above 4°C (39.2°F), the positions reverse, making the deepest water the coolest.

So a little prior knowledge of the relative levels of depth across the bed of a lake or pond, or a little judicious work with the plummet to prove it, should point the angler in the direction of fish. On waters that appear to have an all-over evenness of depth search the bottom carefully. There is bound to be somewhere, be it a very small area, where the depth drops. It may not be by much, but a variation of 0.5m (2ft) or less from the average has been found to be big enough to hold fish.

Wind is another water coolant and provider of oxygen in hot weather besides being a shield to hide the angler from fish that may be lying in the shallows. The stronger the wind the better fish like it and it does not take long for them to show an interest in food. Don't forget that a wind will also drive natural food in front of it, both on and below the surface. Fishing on the windward shore may be a pain because there is a constant need to recast, but it will also be the place where fish could be and you should be prepared to stick it out.

River water keeps a fairly constant temperature and will benefit less from wind than a still water. Water movement itself encourages oxygenation plus cooling, and some current can usually be found, more especially at a weir, but there does not need to be a torrent to interest and hold fish. Watercourses that join a parent water, even small streams, can be attractive and present movement plus perhaps a deeper pool or gully.

Most anglers have cursed boats that charge (has the reader ever seen one going slowly?) up and down our large rivers and reservoirs. But despite our protests those boats provide movement to the water throughout the summer and fish are quite used to their presence. You don't have to fish out in the main navigation channel to find movement – the margins where wash laps the bank sides are equally attractive to many species throughout the day. Especially successful are swims just downstream of locks, where the constant flow of draining water always attracts fish of all species.

Where there is no deep or moving water on a fishery then places which provide shade are at a premium for fish. Weedbeds rank high on the shade front, not only the thick and completely impenetrable stuff which flourishes in great beds but also reed-lined margins that can grow well out from the bank. With suitable tackle fished close to or even through them they can give sport, but beware those same weedbeds at night when they are giving off carbon dioxide and become fish-repellent while so doing.

Bank trees and shrubs not only provide shade for fish, they also often become a source of food as insects and flies fall into the water below. Note that as a rule fish in those situations do not lie out away from the bank. Often they are in the roots below where you are standing and the slightest vibration will put them on guard and off feed. When water is gin clear you would hardly expect fish to seek shade provided by man-made structures, especially those that encourage noise and vibration. Yet they often do. I can think of several bridges over rivers in various parts of the country where even throughout the period of mid-day sun and heat, fish shelter and feed in deep and dark water below the buttresses.

So much for *Where* – now what about *How*? How to approach and how to tackle fish, what tackle to use and how to make sure that it is used with the minimum of disturbance. Boring though it may seem it means starting with the way you approach the water – water craft – and though it has been discussed in an earlier chapter it must be examined again. Polarising glasses to see into the water, soft footwear to cut down vibration on the bank, camouflaged clothing – all have been described.

But you need to go one stage further with camouflage when there is strong light, clear water and low levels. A white human face framed by dark clothing shows clear as a torch to fish on the surface and near to the banks. Blacking up may seem as if it is taking things too far, but it can make the difference between success and suffering the Feast of the Passover. Many keen chub men wear a face mask to avoid just this type of visibility when dapping or slug fishing as a matter of course.

One of the most frustrating occurrences in a drought is to find that fish are occupying a particular stretch of water that is entirely devoid of bankside cover.

When it happens you are left with two choices. If you own the fishing rights and have sole access to the water then it is a simple matter to erect a semi-permanent hide behind which you can creep and from which you can cast. But where the water is a club or a day ticket fishery then possibly the only choice left is to fish at night and hope for the best – providing that fishery rules allow it.

More frustrating are fish that are 'holed up' in safe places and which stay there. Weedbeds are the worst places for this common occurrence, especially large areas of water-lily pads. As water evaporates and the level lowers lily-pads stand higher and higher above the surface. Where once you could cast and 'hang' a bait over a pad to reach fish below there is now no space where the bait could fit.

The only way to deal with fish in that position is to attempt to draw them out with some judicious groundbaiting, no easy job and one without any complete guarantee of success. Search for a clear patch of water adjoining the weed bed around a metre (yard) square. If there is not one then you will have to rake a place clear. Then feed it for two or three successive nights with small amounts of seed or particle type baits such as hemp or rice, or as an alternative, several tiny balls of powdered biscuit crumbs moistened to bind it together. Often these tactics will interest fish and get them to move away from the weeds, possibly because the small amounts that are offered stimulate without providing sustenance.

A sound reason for the lack of success with groundbaits during drought conditions is that when they lie on the bottom, especially if white or light coloured, they make highly visible every fish that might show interest or even patrol in the vicinity. The better method by far is to provide small offerings of your hookbait at sensible intervals spread into a small area around your hook. Fish will not show in silhouette using that method.

One great pest when the water is low can be the humble minnow. They will descend in enormous shoals as your baited hook sinks through the water, or if you are using small amounts of hookbait as loose feed, when it hits the bottom and breaks up. The sheer numbers of these tiddlers effectively block your bait from being seen by better-quality fish, quite apart from providing a constant stream of ridiculous bites to your float. The sensible answer where there is a minnow problem is to keep to heavier and unbreakable baits such as sweetcorn, wheat, etc. that will sink quickly and remain on the bed in one piece.

What other steps can you take to increase your chances during a drought? Using long rods for one. That doesn't imply that they should be used to reach out into the middle of the swim in front of you; the reverse in fact. Use their length to allow you to keep well back from the water, tucked into the bank behind cover and below the skyline. Fine lines go without saying, as do hooks that are in proportion to the hook-bait that is being used. And if you must use a float, then make sure that it is only just heavy enough to cast and as close to being invisible on the water as possible. The recent introduction of floats with clear plastic stems has helped greatly in this direction.

It pays to ring the changes with your hookbaits, more especially the unusual ones that may seem outrageous when compared with some used by run-of-the-mill anglers. My successful 'odd' baits have included freelined and dapped grasshoppers, pieces of saltwater shrimp long-trotted and whole shrimps mounted on a paternoster rig and fished sink-and-draw, maggots dunked in honey after being mounted on the hook, bright-coloured paste baits made with flour and tinted with kitchen dyes or custard powder – the list is as long as your imagination.

But freelining is the method above all others that will bring success when the drought is on. Slugs and snails or balls of cheese, substitute lead swan shot legered and made to work through a gravel run, dapping with both the natural and artificial fly are but a few suggestions. Most of them are discussed in other chapters.

Finally, should water levels drop to their lowest and fishing become utterly impossible then get up on your feet, go to the banks and look, learn, and record what you see. It may be years before you get the chance to see below the water again, so seize the opportunity and take note of underwater obstructions, the

7. A spin-off from drought conditions. This bend produced good fish but lost a lot of tackle in the doing. Very low water during a drought exposed the stakes shown by the arrow, the cause of repeated snagging.

make-up of the bed, the position and length of tree roots and low-growing branches, undercut banks and other snag-filled delights laid bare for you to examine. (See photograph 7.)

Take the camera with you — it need not be an expensive model — and don't forget that black and white can often provide a better record of dark areas than colour prints. Don't throw the prints into a drawer when you get them; enter them in a scrapbook, label and date each one and provide a clue as to where you were standing when the picture was taken. Only by making records like these will you be able to see the various subtle changes that take place on a fishery, many of them brought about by the action of the drought.

Chapter 6

THE RISE AND FALL OF TIDAL FISHING

I quickly became aware of the sin of presumption when I began to fish on the tideways. I started the sport and served my apprenticeship fishing on the Thames, achieving some success in my initial outings. At the end of a year or so I not only imagined that I knew all about the subject, but also decided that tidal fisheries throughout the country would look, behave and fish in exactly the same way. I presumed that the only difference between fresh and tidal fishing came from the action of the tide that altered the water level twice in every 24 hours. It didn't take long for me to realise my mistake and change my mind.

It happened when the half-lock in the Thames at Richmond was being repaired during a very long and hot summer, an occasion that dropped the water level upstream, as far as the barrier formed by the weir at Teddington, below that of the lowest tide which I had ever seen. Until that time I had never bothered to consider what the bed of the river would look like. After I had taken a good, long look at it I not only changed my ideas on where to fish, I also altered my tactics on tideways completely.

With the river reduced to a trickle whole areas become one vast lunar landscape of gravel pockmarked by craters, channels and raised hummocks without weed growth, obstruction or pattern of any description. I saw that swims where I had taken good fish in the past were completely featureless. And just to make matters worse, when I returned two weeks later to fish the new swims that I had marked on a previous visit I found that several days of very high tides had altered the whole geography of the bottom yet again.

The need to understand tides, their pattern and the action that they can produce is vital. Without that knowledge you are condemned to failure. With it can come some of the biggest nets of fish imaginable. In its simplest form there are two high tides during every 24-hour period. The height that these tides reach is governed by the moon, a full moon giving very high tides (springs), with the smaller new moon (which exercises little gravitational pull on seas and oceans) producing a high tide well below that which is normal. Those tides are called neaps. The times of high and low water are shown in local papers or in a tide table that can be purchased from a tackle shop.

High water on the coast will be earlier than high water inland and the tide will take time to back up and reach the saline level, which is the point above which there will be sufficient fresh water to support coarse fish life. As an example the difference between high water at London Bridge and Teddington on the Thames is a little over one hour. Knowing the time of high water is important because you will need to be in position and ready to fish long before it is reached.

The big difference between fishing the tidal as opposed to the non-tidal river is that fish on tideways will have no predetermined feeding areas or patterns. The action of the rising water will stir up the bed, flood over gravel that has been exposed, and generally put fish into a feeding mood. What happens after that is up to the angler.

It is possible to net a bag of excellent roach or dace during a hot summer's day when you would normally not be near the water. I have also obtained the same results on a bitter winter's day when there has been fine snow driving nearly horizontally across the water. But it should be admitted that some species, especially barbel and bream, remain nocturnal in the main and only by fishing over high water after dark will the best results be obtained.

But don't get the idea that tidal fish are always out on suicide missions. They will often feed very intently but only for a very short period, and feeding patterns may vary from place to place, even swim to swim. It is only the man in the right swim and with the right tackle who is in with a fighting chance.

During low water tidal rivers lie well down between the banks flanked by flats. With luck these flats are gravel, which means that the angler can put on his waders, get out onto them and fish. If they are of mud (the Sussex Ouse is an example) then access is not only difficult, but can be dangerous. Fishing when the water is low largely becomes a matter of chuck and chance it. The angler has nothing in the way of cover behind which he can conceal himself and there is often little or no deep water in which to establish a decent swim. Fishing styles are largely restricted to long trotting using the finest tackle possible with fine groundbaits broadcast lightly along the water.

But when the tide turns and the river fills there is a different picture. Shoals of fish will move out from whatever deep water they have been able to find and will drift in with the flood over shallows as they become covered. As the tide increases its flow it will meet the normal downstream flow of freshwater, causing a break up of the current into an enormous number of rolling back eddies, fast glides and slack water. It is in the areas of slack — not dead — water that food which is normally carried by the current will settle and where fish will follow.

Knowing where slack water will form is a major weapon in the armoury of the tidal fishing angler. Not only must he know its exact position, but he must be able to place himself in a position on the bank where he can take advantage of it the moment that the tide turns. That is no easy matter when you stop and think that with water rising quickly one can be flooded out in a matter of minutes. But

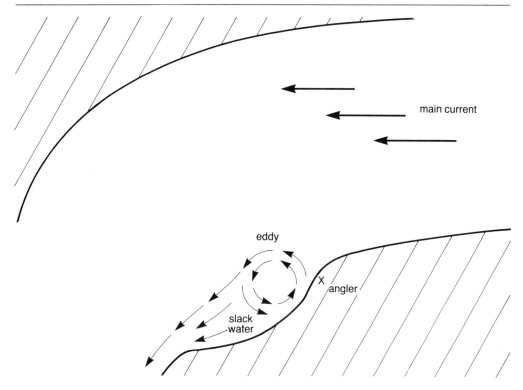

Diagram 2. *An area of slack water away from the thrust of
a rising tide.*

the angler must accept that fate and be prepared to fall back into a predetermined
position from where he can still fish.

One of my favourite and most successful areas of slack water that I fish is
shown in diagram 2. It is on a sharp bend of a river that practically forms a throat
with the opposite bank. The bed is of gravel, totally exposed at times of low water
but as the tide fills then this slowly becomes covered. At half tide the flats are
flooded and it is from that time on that the flow will alter, the main force rushing
through the centre leaving slack water and a slow flow plus an eddy against the
shore line.

Of course the run down of the tide (ebb) after high water presents the reverse
picture, and slack water will be formed on the other side of the bend. There are
occasions when fish will feed as eagerly then as they did during the flood, but
only during the colder months. Receding water and good light makes for
cautious fish that are never far from cover, especially during the summer
months.

So the early part of the tide requires a mobile attack by the angler. Waders, a
good trotting rig with a long rod, fine line and clear-bodied float plus a bait smock
or waist apron with large pockets that can hold more than one type of bait are

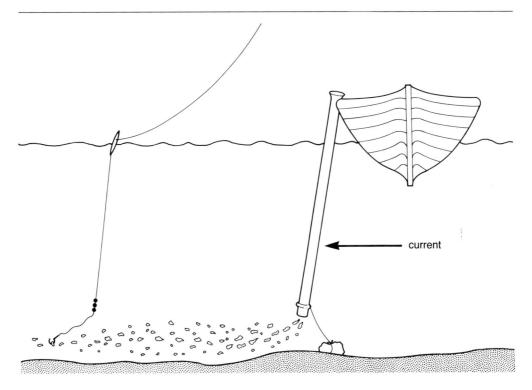

Diagram 3. Piped groundbait from a boat on a tidal water.

essential. Wade to the water's edge leaving tackle box and spare rods safely on the bank. Feed the swim generously with loose offerings of the hookbait – generally maggot – while you swim the stream.

Once the gravel is covered then the final move up to the bank must be made and the angler can settle for about two hours of sport. Now feed the swim with a fast-sinking groundbait as the water deepens and the speed of the current increases, keeping each ball out of any eddies that may form. They will pull particles away and out into the main flow where they will be wasted. Be prepared to bully larger fish once they are hooked to keep them from getting into the current, and increase the size of your hook and link it is tied to if bigger fish, especially bream, appear and start to feed heavily.

Above all, check, counter check and check again the depth between float and bait. Rising water will mean it needs constant adjustment if you don't want to finish up fishing in mid-water among the bleak. Keep a check on line between rod tip and float, holding back so that the bait trips across the bottom ahead of it as it travels downstream. Remember that water at the surface will travel faster than water below it and without that check on the line the float will precede the bait, a situation which allows fish to bite without it registering on the float.

After high water fish will tend to lose their excitement for food. Around this time it sometimes pays to change over to the leger, using a block end feeder loaded with maggots, fished at the end of the swim you have been trotting. Often I have had a good fish – on several occasions the best of the outing – using that method which relies on bigger fish, lying well downstream below the length of travel of the angler's bait, following groundbait particles that wash through a shoal.

The real cream of tideway sport can only come to those who have access to a boat. With it you can remain out in the current during low water where fish will be lying and then position yourself when the tide turns without the bank fisherman's problem of being flooded out. Its use also enables you to groundbait in a highly successful way. Diagram 3 shows the system.

A large funnel is fixed into a length of rigid plastic piping that is lowered over the side of the boat and secured. At the opposite end of the pipe is a length of weighted rope that will keep the end close to the bottom no matter what the state of the tide.

Well-soaked cloud groundbait (when dry it won't sink and will eventually clog the pipe) varied with a little more solid feed as the tide rises, plus occasional maggots or hempseed tipped into the funnel and you have your own ground-baiting machine. With your baited hook dropped over the side you can long-trot to your heart's content – providing that you remember to make those constant adjustments to your float to cope with the varying heights of the tide.

Not all tideways behave in the same way. The Hampshire Avon for instance has a leisurely upstream push of water on a high tide that raises the water level but does not interfere with the main flow other than to slow things down a little. At that time fish always display an increased interest in feeding, especially along the lower stretches of the river as the tide makes, many altering their position into different swims or in the case of mullet grazing the bottom up to an angler's feet seemingly without fear.

One final but little-practised sport on tidal stretches is fly fishing. Dace especially will always take a small, well-presented wet fly on fine tackle, especially at low water. Keep hook sizes down around the 16 mark, use flies under rather than over-dressed, and remember that a small maggot hooked and pushed up around the bend of the hook makes the best fly ever tied even more attractive – especially to bigger dace and roach.

Chapter 7

HOTSPOTS
FACTS AND FICTION

While eavesdropping on a group of match anglers talking after the weigh-in at a competition, I discovered that they were discussing the relative merits and failures of peg numbers along the stretch of river they had been fishing. As they talked I began to realise that they regarded certain pegs as being hotspots, areas which as far as they were concerned gave little chance for fishing failure. If fish were not exactly shoulder to shoulder then at least they were present in good numbers and would feed almost regardless of weather, temperature, water flow or the dozen and one things that normally affect sport – or at least provide reasonably sound excuses should you fail to catch fish.

As they were packing tackle away I asked the winner of the competition (an angler well up in local matchfishing leagues) how he would define a hotspot. You can image my surprise when without hesitation he replied: 'An area in which anglers throw their unused bait and groundbait at the end of the day.'

I had to admit that he was partly right even if the answer did not agree with the mental picture most of us have of hotspots being areas created by nature and not mankind. In fact, several artificially created places immediately come to mind, starting with what is probably the most famous in angling history, Hempseed Corner on the Thames at Hampton Court. Before and immediately after the Second World War anglers dumped hempseed there at the end of the day in such enormous amounts that fish along a quarter-mile stretch would not only ignore other baits, but boil up on the surface if you so much as waved a rod over it. Roach were caught in their hundreds, but on hempseed alone.

Another artificial example is a large reservoir in Essex, renowned for its big pike, which could only be fished along one short stretch of bank. At the end of the day it was not unusual for unused deadbaits to be thrown into the water by departing anglers in quantities large enough to cover a fishmonger's slab.

Naturally it did not take long for a few observant and quick-thinking pike-men to put two and two together and take to fishing after dark, when visiting anglers had gone home and the water had started to settle down from the day's disturbance. Using deadbaits they would invariably come away with at least one or two good fish usually including a specimen in or above the 9kg (20lb) mark.

8. *On the opposite bank can be seen the outline of a stream that at one time drained into the main river – an action that produced a large area of gravel and an angling hotspot.*

More surprising still was that those results invariably came on days when other pike anglers had fished their bite detectors off during the light hours without success of any sort.

But what about natural hotspots? To define one concisely is impossible. No two are ever alike and many would not favour a first, let alone a second glance from an angler. Even when water has been drained from an acknowledged hotspot and the areas around it exposed, there may be nothing to show just what made it so attractive to fish. I know of a featureless swim where current drives heavily against the mud of a concave bend, devoid of weed or shelter and with an even depth throughout but which holds a wonderful head of chub – though heaven knows why! At the other extreme is a plain, straight and uninteresting length of stream that is weeded solid during summer but which gallops through in winter. Against all angling law it produces pike up to 4.5kg (10lb) and sometimes more at regular intervals.

Having said all that it is still possible to recognise the general requirements of a hotspot, the basic background without which they would not exist. But before we

51

examine just what they might be it is probably best to bury rumour, speculation and clap-trap and to get firmly into our heads what they are not. They are not magic pieces of water where fish feed without pause. Unlike artificial hotspots which tend to produce fish with reasonable consistency natural hotspots can go through blank phases without warning and seemingly without reason. Though probably for reasons of ego, we tend to forget the blanks and only remember or boast about the successes!

It is safe to say that hotspots are areas on a fishery — often very small ones at that — which provide food and/or shelter for fish on a regular basis. There is no evidence that the food need be in glut proportions, or that the shelter need be any other than a bush, a few trees, or patch of weed. Hotspots are completely at the mercy of the weather which can affect current, visibility, oxygen content and food levels within or around them. And it is a combination of any or all of those that will not only attract, hold and influence fish, but turn their inclination to feed on or off without reason.

Their location is not related to swims or particular places which anglers may already know and use. But as we have already seen, any one of those known areas can be made into a hotspot within a period of time by the angler's actions. So nothing is easy and nothing can be taken for granted where hotspots are concerned.

Some anglers go to a great deal of trouble in trying to locate a hotspot. Quite a lot of anglers probably know of one already but fail to regard it as such. Far more say that they know one, but when it comes to the crunch it proves to be one whose location has come to them by word of mouth. Hearsay hotspots can be bad news on a fishery. They rarely prove to be prolific (would you tell anyone of a magic swim?) and frequently there is a queue to fish them lasting from morning to night. If they were any good when first discovered they soon become fished out.

If you want to find a hotspot of your own first make sure that you understand the habits, especially the feeding habits, of the species that you want to catch. Next concentrate on the water you intend to fish, not just with a rod in your hand but by walking the banks, taking soundings of the water, studying the current and the position of weedbeds. When you think you really know the water take a pace back and look at the immediate surroundings behind the banks.

At the end of that exercise you should have discovered several new areas where fish may be found and you can settle down to fish them. Don't expect that you will immediately discover a hotspot. What you may have found is a swim or two that produce fish on a very regular basis. If then you concentrate and fish hard you may well find that one swim, and more particularly one small area in a swim, produces fish in bigger sizes and greater numbers than all the others. That is a hotspot.

Why? Perhaps because of the bed. There is ample proof that variations in contours which may occur across the bed of a swim, be the water still or moving, can be vitally important in providing and then keeping a hotspot alive. Deep holes – deep in relation to the rest of the water – not only spell shelter but also safety.

Understanding the geological make-up of the bed, whether it be mud, gravel, silt or sand, is vitally important. One small patch of gravel or sand among a desert of mud and sludge is often all that is needed to attract and hold fish: find that and you have found success. Often such areas stand out a mile when you take a detached look at the swim's surroundings. Photograph 8 is a good example. Study the background and you will notice that in the field behind the bank there are sunken lanes that at first sight might be taken for footpaths.

Actually, they are the courses of old streams which fed into the river at one time, but which dried out and then filled in with the passage of time. Where they eventually linked and joined the main flow, shown by a dip in the bank in the foreground, they carried a considerable amount of gravel into the river over the years, and the gravel remains to this day, the only such area in a long stretch both up and down stream, and a grand hotspot for roach.

9. These old bank supports are used by fish, vertebrates and insects of all types as a breeding area. Eggs and young life are prolific during the summer months and fish feed heavily on them.

Obstructions in the water are famous for providing hotspots, especially those of the 'one fish at a time' variety. A fallen tree, large boulder or old bank support becomes the place for a decent-sized fish to lie, protected from the current and in a position to accept whatever food passes. Once it has been caught a replacement fish of similar size will move in and take up residence, often within a matter of hours.

Undercut banks are notorious hotspots – and places in which tackle may be lost. So too are the classic places referred to in angling literature such as camp sheathing and cattle drinks. Photograph 9 shows a primitive form of bank protection similar in effect to camp sheathing. It is a highly productive hotspot but only at the opening of the season. Why? Because at that time it is a spawning area where fish, invertebrates and insects deposit their eggs. As few fish refuse spawn, be it their own or that of other species, it is never without feeding fish of one sort or other.

Some hotspots have been created by industry and commerce, famous ones usually centring around warm-water returns. The return at Kingston Power Station on the Thames at Canbury Gardens produced a glut of big carp some years ago, while several factories along our canal systems today return warmed water and provide the odd hotspot. Possibly the oldest warm-water hotspot in the country is on the River Avon just below Poultney Bridge with its weir at Bath, where warm water from the Roman Baths is released to produce a well-known pike hold.

But nature can provide natural warm-water hotspots, even though they may be seasonal and confined only to still waters. In Chapter 5, Breaking the Drought, we acknowledged that water temperature was influenced by the weather and that warm and cold water would separate, the warm lying on the surface above that which was cooler during summer months. That level will remain constant until there is a wind which will then tilt the levels and push the warm water towards the lee (down wind) shore. Diagram 4 shows this and the effect it will produce.

Carried with that warm water will be insect life of every sort, both live and drowned, either on the surface or just below it. Fish will move after it and then lie and feed along the bank, protected from view by surface ripple. Naturally hotspots provided by that pattern will only last until there is a change of weather or wind. My local trout reservoir has just such an area during the summer months when wind blows warm water against the hot concrete of the dam wall, bringing a wealth of insects with it and a certain limit of fish for the angler. Yes, it means casting into the wind and approaching the area with extreme care if you don't want to disturb fish. But as I have already said, fish in hotspots are never

OPPOSITE
10. Poultney Bridge and Weir at Bath, Avon. Opposite the anglers is the warm-water outlet from the Roman Baths, a well-known pike hotspot.

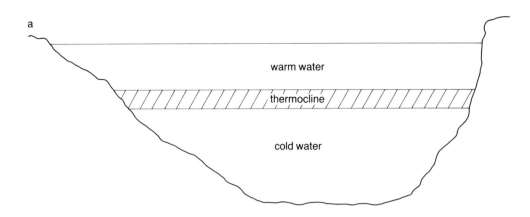

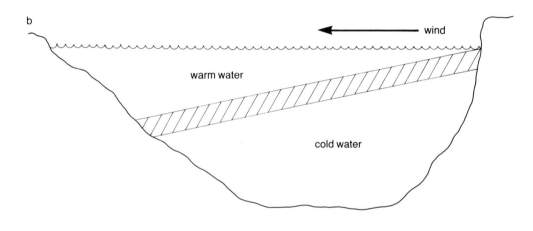

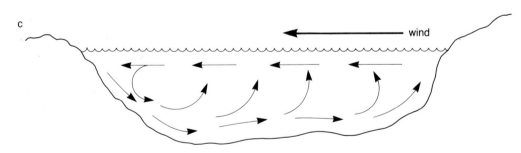

Diagram 4.
a. The area of warm water in a deep lake during summer.
b. Wind tilting warm water to the windward shore, making
a temporary hotspot.
c. Circulation of water in a shallow pond produced by wind.
The best fishing will be on the windward shore.

11. Drab, uninspiring in the extreme – but the arrow points to a first-rate hotspot, though for no obvious reason.

blessed with suicidal desires and always keep their natural caution and cunning.

Hotspots are more likely to occur in rivers and streams than in still waters, and current is largely responsible both for their creation and continuance. Clear channels or patches among thick weedbeds can prove to be hotspots with fish waiting in the shelter for food to wash into clearings. Once located those areas should be sparingly groundbaited and made to produce even better results.

Some of the more frustrating hotspots in running water are those which, when exposed through the action of drought or work by a River Authority as they lower the level of a river or stream, show no abnormal or outstanding features of any sort. I mentioned one earlier in the chapter, and photograph 11 shows another. The plain, uninteresting far bank produced excellent fish on a regular basis for years, and it continued to do so when the water level was restored again, some six months after the photograph was taken. But for no obvious reason.

Eddies and lay-bys produced by holes or subsidence in the banks, or the action of water circulating from the lasher of a weir, are other places that can be hotspots, caused possibly by food circulating along, then being drawn into an area that is sheltered from the main stream. On the same lines are the downstream tails of islands, locks, moored boathouses and other places past which the current will glide, allowing fish shelter and leaving them with the need for the minimum expenditure of energy to collect passing food.

If there is any clear message to be found in this chapter on hotspots it must be that none of them, regardless of size or position, is ever infallible. Changes may occur which are beyond the control of the angler; currents may alter direction or suddenly be diverted through them, silt or mud may be deposited because of current changes, weed beds may die and not grow again – all are beyond the angler's control. It is the short-sighted angler who loses out in the long run, who immediately gives them up or who divulges their position to his friends thinking that they are finished. Dead though the hotspot may appear, there is every chance that it may be resurrected in the future.

Chapter 8

MULLET

THE ANGLING MYTH

'Uncatchable' is the mildest word I have heard when an angler has been describing the mullet – and I have heard plenty of them in my time. They are one of the most infuriating fish that the angler can meet, slipping into view with the current and disappearing just as easily, usually during the time taken to work out a plan of attack. Even nick-names used to describe mullet are derogatory and include Grey Ghosts, an obvious reference to their ability to haunt a stretch of water, and Whitelips, derived from the thick chub-like mouth that shows exceptionally well when fish are in shallow water. Without exception all other descriptions that I have heard have been unprintable.

Why have myths and legends grown around this species describing it as being nearly uncatchable? Possibly because anglers see a mullet swimming in the river and then try to catch that particular fish instead of concentrating on the species as a whole. Partly also because they rate them as being possessed with exactly the same temperaments and habits as a freshwater fish.

There are three species of this saltwater fish that are found in British waters. They are the thick-lipped grey mullet, the commonest species which inhabits all waters round our coast and which can reach weights upwards of 4.5kg (10lb), the thin-lipped grey, a smaller species, generally found on the south coast of England, and the rare golden grey mullet.

Although most of their time is spent at sea, mullet will take to estuaries, tidal creeks and harbours, many of them working inland along tidal sections of rivers where they may travel upstream for very long distances. Though not capable of taking total residence, they can exist in fresh water for some time. Their excursions away from the coast take place during the summer months and it is then, when water is clear, that anglers become aware of their presence.

Mullet are bottom scavengers, sucking up mud and sand from the bed from which they extract diatoms and tiny insect life. Once food has been extracted the waste is expelled, leaving evidence of their work in the shape of lines and raised channels cutting across the bed.

Difficult though these fish may be labelled they are creatures of habit and can, over a period of time, be conditioned into feeding and taking a bait. They quickly

12. Pieces of shrimp and prawn make excellent bait for mullet.

'learn' to ignore holidaymakers and workers along harbour walls and to a lesser extent people (anglers included) along the banks of tidal rivers. Naturally inquisitive, they will stop and cautiously inspect anything that is in their path, providing that it does not immediately arouse their suspicions. And an interested mullet is one well on the way to being hooked.

Fishing must start long before the tide flows, when the bed between the river banks is exposed at low water. Armed with a pair of waders and a small fork the angler must dig out small mud ragworm that live in exposed mud flats. Store them in damp sand that will not only keep them alive but also help to toughen them. It can be hard and messy work but those tiny, fragile worms, which often fragment when you handle them, are the mullet bait supreme.

Many other baits have had varying degrees of success over the years with some of the more outlandish ones achieving local rather than national fame. They have included bread, earthworms of various sorts, paste, fish flesh, maggots, caster, green peas, sweetcorn, banana cubes and pieces of shrimp.

Fish that are caught without the angler having groundbaited well in advance are literally Gifts from the Gods. To ensure repeated success it is necessary to provide a steady trail of ultra-fine food such as breadcrumbs or, farther down the river and close to the estuary itself, fish scraps.

White breadcrumbs reduced to powder will sink slowly in a cloud, and when pilchard oil has been added will trail a scent stream along the current which will attract and hold mullet. There are variations on that theme and I have seen bran, porridge (both cooked and uncooked) and crushed sausage rusk all with or without the addition of pilchard oil being used. Choose the places where you use it carefully. Study fish movements over the period of a couple of high tides and then bait up four or five different swims spaced well apart, starting when the tide begins to make and continuing until the first fish are seen nosing upstream with the current.

Mullet like to keep on the move and although they may seem appreciative of a good groundbait trail, they may suddenly and without reason leave. With several other places prepared you can usually hope to attract and hold them again.

Fish offal such as broken-up plaice bones and fish heads attract mullet by scent as much as from any actual food value. It is usual to moor them to the bottom secured in a hair net, upstream of where it is intended to fish. To reap the full benefit of this system it is advisable to bait for several days in advance to get mullet used to the free feed. In water with a strong tidal flow it is better to pack the bait into a tin with a perforated lid, burying this at low water but leaving the lid showing above the mud so that the incoming tide will wash food particles and more especially scent through the water.

The fact that mullet in the upper reaches of a tideway can be caught at the same time and with the same tackle as freshwater fish is probably the reason why so many anglers blank out. The mullet gets to take second place behind coarse fish and only receives serious consideration when one is actually seen cruising around the swim – a sight that immediately galvanises the angler into taking all the wrong actions.

If you want to catch mullet then think mullet. Use the longest rod possible which will provide you with line control, reduce the physical effort of casting and allow you to keep well back and away from the skyline. The skyline is the undoing of many would-be mullet fishers who don't appreciate that in the clear water of a rising tide fish will not only see his outline through the surface but also his shadow as it falls onto the river bed itself. Yes, mullet *can* become conditioned to people on the bank – but not when they wave a fishing rod all over the place.

Long trotting will undoubtedly be your best bet on most days that you fish, with special emphasis on the word 'long'. The normal trot is 9m (10 yards) or more, with up to 18m (20 yards) being needed to come to terms with shy fish that are hanging on at the end of the swim for groundbait missed by others that are feeding. That means using a fine line – around 0.9kg (2lb) in breaking strain or a little above – and a fixed float large enough to cope with the current, weighted low to record the slightest touch from a fish. Clear plastic is good, but to prevent glint being given off from its body rub it down with a little wet-and-dry emery paper to give a matt finish.

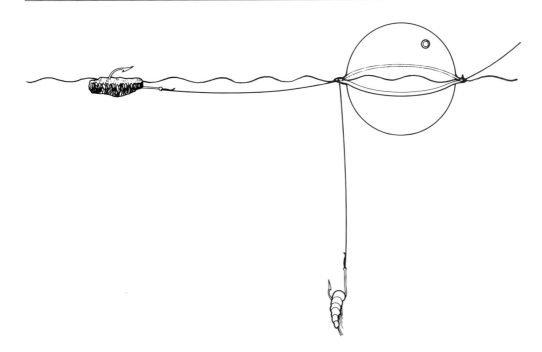

Diagram 5. *A two hook rig for shallow water fished with the aid of a bubble float.*

Keep it on the move up and down the line to cope with the changing depths that the tide will bring. Fish with fine wire hooks in sizes well in keeping with both size and type of bait that is being used, tied to a 0.5kg (1lb) breaking strain link. That sounds suicidal and without skill and patience on the part of the angler when he plays the fish it most certainly will be. But there is a maxim for mullet which runs 'Big hooks, big blanks'.

Skill, patience and restraint will not only be needed when a fish is being played, but will have to be observed when the strike is made. All members of the mullet family have a very fine membrane behind the lip which is easily torn so pull the hook home as opposed to banging it in, and then be prepared to give the fish its head without bullying. Once the lip is torn or even if the hook should enlarge its grip through the membrane surrounding it you can say goodbye to the fish.

There are times when mullet feed in water so shallow that the normal float-fished rig cannot get close to them. Often this will happen at low tide – when there is little water in the river and fish are confined to its seaward end. You can get to them by preparing a rig that uses a bubble float secured in the normal surface-fishing style presenting a bait at the surface, together with the addition of a dropper half-way between float and hook just long enough to bump a bait across the bottom (see diagram 5).

You now have the chance to fish with two different baits which can be alternated, starting perhaps with flake on the end hook and, say, shrimp on the dropper. Make your cast well upstream so that the splash of its landing will not disturb fish, let it work easily through the swim and then gently hold the float back, bringing it to the bank at your feet ready to be retrieved. For obvious reasons, under no circumstances should you attempt to retrieve the rig by pulling it through the centre of the swim.

Mullet are occasionally drawn to weed-covered walls, piles and other underwater supports. They will browse on the growing hair weed which is too fine to collect and fix onto a hook. To attempt to get at the fish by dropping a baited hook from the bank immediately above them is to put every one of them down. But they can often be coaxed into accepting a bait supported by a small piece of cork with one small lead-substitute shot pinched below it, made to drift downstream from a position well above where they are lying. Again the bait is not so important as the approach, but bread either in paste or flake form, possibly with a drop of pilchard oil, can work wonders.

One final method of attack is worth remembering. Mullet are attracted by bright lights of any sort. Not just the light from a night fisherman's torch or lamp, but permanent lights, especially street lights, that flank the river. It is always worth night fishing in such an area on a rising tide, long trotting and using light-coloured hookbaits, especially maggot, combined with a slow-sinking groundbait. Keep repeated watch on the depth and be prepared to find that fish will be just as anxious to feed on the ebb as on the flood.

Chapter 9
MARSHES
AN ANGLING CHALLENGE

It needs a special breed of angler who can fish the flat, open marshes of this country with repeated success. Each vast tract of land laced with waterways differs according to its location, but they all possess basic features that create a challenge of their own. For years they were ignored by anglers other than a few who lived close at hand. Now large stretches are in demand throughout the season, more especially by matchmen who travel miles to visit them. They are the masters of the waterway while they fish all-in to fill a keepnet. But it takes a special approach to come to terms with the big fish with which many marsh ditches and drains are blessed.

Studied from the air marshes look like the skeleton of a fish that has been opened and filleted. Large canal-type waterways, the main drains, cut across the land each terminating at the sea. Leading from each of the main drains is a series of smaller guts and dykes, diminishing in size until they become tiny ditches. They have the initial task of carrying away surplus water from the flat, boggy land.

Viewed from the ground marshes seem dull and placid, but they are far from that. Both long- and short-term changes are constantly occurring, many of which affect the angler of today. Many more will affect the angler of the future, largely through problems that arise from rapid alterations in agricultural use.

Marshes were once grazing ground for cattle, but now vast tracts are being reclaimed for cereal growing. To do this demands that mile after mile of surface drains be laid across the land to carry away water. Unfortunately those drains don't only carry water, they also carry tons of silt that serve to choke and clog drains and dykes into which they feed.

But that is not the end of the story. After drainage comes the plough, followed by the spreading of tons of artificial fertilisers. Those fertilisers, which must ultimately leech into the drainage system, are the last straw, causing weed growth to be stimulated to such a degree that it spreads from bank to bank.

So much for encroachment that will face the angler of tomorrow. There are many other problems facing those who fish today, the most important centring on water levels and how they are controlled along the various waterways. The principle is simple: small ditches drain into bigger dykes and drains which in turn run to the main watercourses. By design those big waters have high banks, and at regular intervals pumps are installed to lift water from the smaller courses into them. When they start to fill they in turn must be drained either by sluice or by pump into the sea.

This means that in winter, especially when there is high rainfall, there can be a constant shift of water levels going on. It may happen when the angler is fishing, producing a sudden draw on the water, it may happen well beforehand with the Water Authority anticipating heavy rain and dropping the water level throughout the system practically to summer drought level. There is seldom any warning, and the angler should be prepared for extremes by the hour. During summer the reverse often occurs and pumps remain silent, waterways lie utterly unprotected against the sun, and water quickly evaporates. That in turn will trigger weed growth to such an extent that it will make many smaller waterways nearly unfishable.

Silt is another hazard for the angler. It will settle out of the water and be reinforced by rotting weed in the course of a few seasons, filling the bottom of waterways, especially the smaller ones where there may be little hard draw and current. Dredging is the only treatment for that condition. It is a relentless and ongoing task that without warning will not only remove a favourite swim the angler intended to fish but also alter the whole stretch of water in which it was contained.

Yet another problem that the marshes can produce for an angler is wind. Not just high winds, but severe gales that can blow for days on end across the flat, open spaces, often driving snow and rain before it. No great difficulty if you are fishing on one of the main drains where you can get down under the shelter of the bank – providing that the wind is not blowing up or down stream.

But if you want to fish one of the dykes or ditches then shelter is vital – but at a premium. During the past 20 years or so some bankside growth, especially hawthorn bushes and willow trees, has been allowed to flourish or has even been planted in some parts of the country. But by and large the angler must provide his own protection, and pretty strong stuff at that.

Now let's recap on the general problems that face the angler who sets out to fish on the marsh. These are heavy weed growth, extremes in water levels and movement of current, dredging, and lack of cover. By keeping to the main channels it is possible that you might occasionally be able to avoid some of them. But move to the smaller dykes where some of the best fish are to be found and you must learn how to beat or avoid them.

If you have not got a sensible rake with enough weight to hold bottom and take weed out by the roots then you won't stand a chance of beating it and getting to grips with the tench, carp and bream which are plentiful on the smaller channels. Look for swims at or close to the junction of one channel with another

13. One of the main drains on a marsh, wide to the skies and without shelter of any sort. Fine during the summer months, but a different 'kettle of fish' during winter.

where there may be a greater depth, and don't clear everything out of the water that you can see. A small clearing with a weed bed left on either side of the swim will provide necessary cover for fish that you will be hoping to attract by pre-baiting.

One particular weed haunts the marshes every summer, providing little or no chance of control. It is duckweed, the green carpet menace that spreads over all waters that are unprotected from the sun. There is no beating it, but every chance of finding a small stretch – perhaps only a tiny patch – of clear water on the bigger drains, where wind and a little surface movement will break the covering. Study the weather and above all be mobile when the curse is at its height.

Shifting water levels during autumn and winter months can be a mixed blessing. Sometimes things are carried to extremes by the River Authorities and there may only be 0.6–0.9m (2–3ft) where normally there is 3m (10ft), in which case you must shop around the marsh for a drain or dyke that has been left full. But pump action can be very much to the angler's advantage. You don't have to be in the main blast of water below the outlet; far better is to get above the pump so that there is a gentle draw rather than a hard push to the current.

An artificial flow can be an enormous blessing on flat days, especially on those cold morning when the water is gin clear and fish won't respond to anything that may be offered by way of hookbait, no matter how many changes are tried. The pull of water is enough to disturb the bed, and that is often enough to start fish feeding.

Because a particular stretch of water carries a certain amount of silt it will not necessarily follow that it won't hold fish. Fish, sometimes good ones, are quite at home on drains and dykes often only 0.9m (3ft) or less in depth. I sometimes think that the silting action is so gradual that they don't notice its effects. But fishing on those shallow waters is all a matter of timing, in this particular case the time that you choose to fish. Try it in bright sunlight or after a biting frost and you will be doomed to failure. Fish early, late, or in subdued light, keeping well back from the bankside and freelining a natural bait and you will make your mark.

The common interpretation that anglers give to dredging activities is that for several seasons to come that particular length of water will be devoid of fish, but that may not be strictly true. Within days, sometimes only a single day, fish will be back, working along the now clear bottom looking for and finding food in abundance. Especially high on their food list will be leeches and water snails which will have been dragged or shaken from weedbeds in high numbers.

I trace the course dredgers take and try to fish on selected stretches as soon as the water has settled. Visiting them too soon can lead to problems if the silt has not settled from the water, a frequent summer happening that obscures the bait. In winter mud dredged and dumped on the banks can make them a quagmire, completely unapproachable by the angler. There have been occasions when I have waited six months and even then been unsuccessful on a freshly dredged stretch. But when eventually the water settles I score with a vengeance, making the waiting well worth while.

Cover from the worst of the weather must be a big consideration if you are to graduate as an all-seasons marsh angler. Sitting on a flat bank with a Force 7 gale nearly blowing you into the water will do nothing to aid your concentration and that, as we have decided earlier, is nine-tenths of successful fishing.

Along the main channels it is often possible to tuck down into clumps of reed mace and get some cover from the wind. On other stretches natural growth, bushes and so on, will give some protection from the wind. But out in the open there is only one possible comfort that I know of, and that is to make your own wind break. It may be nothing more than a large black refuse sack slid over two garden canes pushed well into the ground to hold it open, but it is surprising just how much wind and rain that lightweight shelter can keep off.

In recent years there have been some excellent pike reported from marsh drains all over the country. In many cases the exact location where many of these fish have been caught has been 'moved' by the time the report reaches the angling press in an effort to keep pressure off a particular water. Nature has a backhanded way of getting its own back on anglers, and often some of those imagined places of capture do actually produce fish when the newspaper-reading hunters turn up in their droves to try their luck.

Pike in the smaller drains are often lone specimens which occasionally reach double-figure weight. Those that inhabit the main drains often make double figures and tend to shoal along a particular reach. There appears to be no apparent reason for this habit. The topography of the bank, its depth, weed growth, etc, are all the same as on any other stretch of water. And to further cloud the issue the shoal may have moved completely within a month, or by the time that the next season opens − frequently into an area that is just as featureless.

Keep mobile when you fish for pike. Ring the changes on rigs and baits, especially smaller baits such as sprat, smelt, and sardine. Don't forget that providing your tackle is in balance it is possible to plug-fish and spin even small waters. That includes the summer months when a deadbait is not only acceptable to fish but not an expensive loss should it become snagged on the weeds.

Above all keep a diary and log the where, when and how of fish of all species that you take. In particular describe the weather both on the days of success and when you blank out. You may well have the 'feel' for a particular stretch and it's an odds-on chance that fish will be there. But with some background of knowledge you will have a head start on how to tackle them.

Chapter 10
ALL-ROUND RUDD

During very many years spent fishing I can only recall finding five waters that contained rudd. Pure rudd that is, not the hybrids that seem to inhabit half the fisheries of the British Isles today. And of those five only two contained fish that could average 0.4kg (1lb) and more, the remainder being over-populated with fish that never exceeded 140g (5oz) at the most. This was not the fault of the rudd, but the surroundings in which they lived.

To reach any size and to keep a pure strain rudd need a large water with plenty of shallows as well as some deep holes, an abundance of weed and an ample supply of food. Even when supplied with this they will breed at an enormous rate and may eventually reduce themselves to a stunted population. Both of the fisheries I use that produce good rudd are medium-sized private lakes well off the beaten track, and both hold a good head of pike. Their presence keeps a balance and stops breeding from getting out of hand, and this, coupled with the fact that there are no roach or bream in the lakes with which rudd can hybridise, produces pure rudd of a decent size and weight.

On waters with a large head of small rudd the fish are suicidal, throwing themselves onto any hook baited with a small, preferably light-coloured bait. On water where there are large fish there is a totally different picture. Fish will be shy and alert, moving in large shoals that contain a complete range of sizes. Normally they patrol the edges quite close to the banks, working through weed and reed growth. But once disturbed they will head for deep water or the centre of a lake, often hiding there for the remaining hours of daylight.

Angling books make much of the fact that rudd have an undershot lower lip which makes them surface feeders, and that anglers should direct their attention to the top of the water. In practice, rudd have no difficulty in feeding off the bottom by 'snouting', driving their mouths under the bed and then extracting food from it, feeding in a similar manner to mullet.

Another old wives' tale that clings to rudd fishing is that you should throw crusts of bread onto the surface in front of you to attract fish and entice them into feeding before freelining a bait in that area. This works but unfortunately it also brings the smallest fish to the top, better fish being crowded out and remaining below the surface.

Surface fishing with freelined bread or breakfast cereal baits (there are many varieties on the market now conveniently shaped into squares and circles that float) will take fish without groundbait of any sort. But by concentrating on the surface alone the angler will miss the chance to get at bigger fish which will be congregated below those feeding above them. Better by far to feed very occasional pellet-sized balls of cloud groundbait that will break up the moment that it hits the water.

At irregular intervals during the day tactics can be changed to fishing on the drop. The smallest self-cocking float can be added to the line with one lead substitute dust shot above the hook. It will allow the bait to sink slowly through surface fish to reach those below that are probably of a bigger size. Small amounts of loose hookbait can be thrown or catapulted around the float and the occasional tiny ball of cloud bait added into the swim.

Eventually, better fish still will be taken by fishing a bait on the bottom, either by means of a shot leger or by laying-on. It will pay to fish a bigger bait and larger hook, up to size 10, and to strike not only when the float dips, but when it makes sideways movements. Big rudd frequently pick up a bait from the bottom and turn on their sides at the same time, possibly because of the position of their mouth.

Once the surface temperature drops rudd will move to deeper water. They become hard to locate on big waters, giving anglers no option but to move around trying the deeps until they are discovered. One possible solution is to fish into the wind, especially if that wind happens to be warm. Once discovered and providing that the water is not gin clear they can often be brought on feed with a light breadcrumb or sausage rusk mix garnished with white maggots. They also appreciate a cocktail hookbait, favourites being paste or crust with a maggot capping tucked behind the barb.

Rudd feed well at night, and on large waters this is one sure way of getting to grips with big fish. They will surface feed without fear and a freelined bait kept close to the margins of weeds or especially rush-lined banks is the best and most successful approach. Crust is by far the best bait, using larger pieces than you would offer during the day on hooks up to size 6 or 8.

Loose pieces of crust can help bring fish on feed at night without quite as much risk of bringing small specimens to the surface as so often happens during the day. It will also pay to change the size of your line into one of a higher breaking strain. More than one large tench or carp has surprised an angler only expecting to catch rudd. Keep a slack line between bait and rod tip which will prevent fish from sucking it away from the hook. Where this happens on a regular basis – and some rudd seem to have got hook stripping to a fine art – it pays to make a cocktail of several maggots mounted on either side of the crust.

One peculiarity of the rudd is its attraction to a moving bait. This movement can be from a surface-fished bait, perhaps induced by the wind, or a bottom-fished bait dragged very slowly by the angler. It is a tip worth remembering when

14. *You do not need to be an expert fly-fisherman to catch rudd.*
These were taken on a coachman.

sport seems to go off. It is also the reason why rudd will take both fly and spinner.

You do not need to be the perfect fly-fisherman to take rudd. Long casts are not necessary 9–18m (10–20 yards) normally being enough to reach fish. Far more important is an ability on the part of the angler not to show himself against the skyline, and to use light tackle. A rod capable of handling a dark-coloured size 6 floating line is ideal.

Cheats prosper where fly fishing for rudd is concerned, those who are toffee-nosed and mindful of the rules always losing out! Start fly fishing by watching where fish are moving and then cast to them in the normal way. Flies that are successful include the Palmer family with big bushy bodies, Coachman, White Moth – in fact anything that looks like a reasonably natural insect which would land on the water during a warm day.

Don't worry too much if the line does not make a thistle-down landing on the water. Providing that fish cannot see you they will probably drop below the surface for a few moments before returning. If there is a wind and the line drags then so much to the good, a moving bait (as we have already discussed) is not a bad thing in rudd fishing.

If there are no signs of feeding fish then to hell with tradition and do the sensible thing. Take your catapult and throw out a pouchful of maggots, spread well over the surface. Keep up the good work until fish are seen to be interested, then offer them your fly. Ten to one it will be taken immediately with a firm swirl, the fish hooking itself as it turns away with the fly in its mouth.

If fish are wary of the fly then tuck a maggot up under the barb and try again. That should get them – and if it doesn't then take the fly off and fish instead with two or three maggots mounted on a size 12 hook. Yes, it is freelining, but you won't cast a bait as light as that without the aid of a heavy line.

One other ruse is well worth trying, and one that will often produce the best fish. Take your fly and squeeze a lead substitute dust shot onto the cast immediately above the eye. Now cast and allow the fly to sink before retrieving back to you in a sink-and-draw motion. Take your time before starting to work the fly; the weight will make it sink slowly and you should aim at letting it get at least 0.6m (2ft) or more below the surface. You won't score at every cast using this method, but the waiting until you do will not prove to have been time wasted.

Talk of moving baits for rudd must prompt the question of spinning. Yes, they will take the spinner and take it well. One particular trait of their feeding cycle is to gorge on spawn during the early months of the year, not just that of other fish but their own as well. But their interest in a spun bait is not restricted just to that time; it holds through the summer months and into autumn.

There is little sense in using a proper spinning rod for rudd. The fly rod will do as well, probably better, being responsive at the tip and working throughout its length. It is possible to use the fly line, but I prefer to change to a closed face or fixed-spool reel with a line of 1.3kg (3lb) b.s., and more where there is a considerable amount of weed to contend with.

Spinners must not be large. Fly spinners in both copper and silver are ideal, so are the extra-small leaf spinners on the market with a weighted body. Use the lightest for shallow water and the heavier models for deep holes. The normal straight retrieve will take fish providing that it is not too fast. Better, especially on waters that are well weeded, is to work the heavier spinners in a sink-and-draw style.

Don't strike hard when a fish takes – the hook will be in contact with a very soft lip area and can tear out in seconds, and do not bully a fish into the landing net. If it manages to weed itself keep an even strain on the line and wait. Jerking will tear the hook from the mouth of the fish and into the weed, making sure that the spinner will be lost. Keeping up the strain and waiting patiently will eventually make the fish move.

Again, there are a few useful tricks that can be used to make the spinner more attractive when fish seem to be uninterested. A thin strip of silver paper around 5cm (2in) long attached to one hook on a treble so that it will trail along through the water behind is a dodge I have successfully employed. Possibly the fish feels that the silver paper represents something already in pursuit of the bait, so grabs it immediately rather than run the risk of losing it.

Yet another method is to hook small redworms onto the treble, several on each hook so that a bunch seems to be moving through the water. Quite why this should cause interest I don't know. I have had success with a spinner baited in this way when a worm fished normally or retrieved slowly through the water has not brought success. It is all in keeping with the image of the rudd, an attractive species that provides all-round sport.

Chapter 11

BAITING AND RAKING

You do not need a magic formula to produce successful groundbait although you might think so. In fact if you study the description and claims printed on some of the plastic bags holding proprietary groundbaits stacked on shelves in tackle shops, you will be left in no doubt that not only is such an elixir essential, it is also completely unobtainable – other than in the bag offered for sale.

The fact is that we anglers are not only gullible where groundbait is concerned but suspicious and superstitious into the bargain. You hear stories on the subject every day most of which centre on the fact that when old so-and-so fishes he always gets a net-full regardless of the water or the weather, and he is successful perhaps because of the special groundbait he uses.

Well, it is probably true that so-and-so is highly successful. But there are dozens of others like him who also succeed. And you can take it from me that none of them owes it to super ingredients that are added to their groundbait. The secret of their success lies in the fact that they have taken time and trouble to study and understand the what, where, when, why and how of making, mixing and then feeding groundbait into the swim that they fish.

If you want to follow in their footsteps start by learning the basic aims and objects. These state that groundbait is used

1. To interest fish on small waters
2. To attract fish on large waters
3. To hold fish in any type of water once they have been collected.

Notice that there is no provision, or even suggestion, that fish should be fed; in fact the word 'feed' hardly ever occurs except for one or two species that are gross eaters and which will be dealt with separately.

Now for the actual make-up of groundbait itself. The materials used must depend on the type of water that will be fished. Generally, a cloud type, made from very fine particles that will break up and slowly fall through the water, should be used on still waters. Heavy stodge, pudding stuff that will sink like lead and then cling to the bottom, should be used on fast-moving waters. Where the movement of water is exceptionally fast it may be necessary to add extra weight to take groundbait to the bottom, and what is used need not necessarily be an attraction to fish.

The basis for most groundbait mixes is bread in one form or another, either dried and crushed into crumbs or left in its natural loaf form. It attracts fish by colour, taste and to a lesser degree 'smell'. If there is any 'magic' in groundbait then it must stem from the manner in which this very basic ingredient is prepared, coupled with certain other possible attractors used to increase both visibility and taste.

Breadcrumbs can be purchased in bulk from tackle shops. But there are still enthusiasts who dry bread in the oven and crush it with the aid of a mincer and then a food blender to make their own cloud bait. Their object is to produce a pure white mix, something that can be difficult to purchase from a shop. A large proportion of proprietary baits on offer have other ingredients added, some I have noticed being clearly labelled 'Unfit for human consumption'.

As far as I am concerned if it is not good enough for me to eat then fish should not be offered it, and because of this I continue (with many others of like mind) to make my own. Breadcrumbs from a fishmonger's shop are pure and provide a ready-made alternative, but they have a yellow additive. They need putting through a blender to produce a cloud type powder. Fish find them attractive — providing that they are used on the right water. Use on a swim that has a gravel bed is not recommended for obvious reasons unless of course pre-baiting has taken place over a succession of days, allowing fish time to discover them.

There are many other materials that will produce a cheap and effective cloud bait. Sweet biscuits and cheese biscuits are two that make a light-coloured bait with increased taste and smell. Dog biscuits provide many others in a host of colours, especially those which have a meat basis such as 'Go Pup.' They are cheap, work exceptionally well and only need crushing or blending into crumb or powder form.

Two schools of thought exist when it comes to producing solid groundbait. One maintains that bread used as the base should be scalded and then mixed at home. The other is emphatic that groundbait of any sort should be mixed on the bank, using water taken from the swim. I mix mine, either cloud or solid, on the spot, not because I think that fish can tell tap from untreated water, but because dry groundbait of any sort is lighter to carry.

Soaked bread is likely to be sloppy and may need stiffening, especially when it is needed to sink immediately to the bottom. Bran is the universal mixer, although ground dog biscuit, sausage rusk, sand and mud are just a few of the other stiffening and quick-sinking agents that can be used. One mixing agent that I favour is boiled and crushed potato. It is heavy, does little actually to feed the fish and adds whiteness, something vitally important when coloured water and floods are fished.

Many anglers add a little of their hookbait to their groundbait in an effort to accustom fish to it. It can be a retrograde step, especially if too much is used, feeding rather than attracting them. But there is much to be said for adding fluid

15. If a heavy groundbait is absolutely necessary, it is easier to carry it dry and then mix it on the bankside.

in which some of the hookbaits have been prepared, e.g. hemp, wheat, or the juice out of sweetcorn tins into either cloud or solid bait.

What of the many 'special' additives described as being 'for roach' or 'for bream' that you read about on the packets holding shop-bought baits? Take your choice and then make your own decision. My experience, and that of dozens of other anglers including many well up on the match circuit, is that 'special' additives can be one-off gimmicks that succeed on the odd water or on a day when conditions are just right. But overall they don't account for a great deal. If the bait you have prepared is simple, fresh and capable of providing the type of attraction you are looking for then it will be successful.

There is a large and growing school of thought that refuses to offer bulk groundbait of any sort. Instead small offerings of whatever bait is on the hook will be fed into the swim in controlled amounts, perhaps a dozen or so maggots to start with at every swim down when long trotting, or every four or five minutes when fishing a still water. Once fish are on the feed and it becomes obvious that there is a fair-sized shoal of them then amounts can be increased to keep them in the swim. I can think of no more sensible way of groundbaiting for the majority of species.

Presentation is everything, and little and often must be the watchword. Little amounts encourage fish without committing the crime of feeding them. 'Often' means regulating the frequency with which you offer groundbait. A little thrown in at rapid intervals will soon add up to a lot, and that leads to overfeeding. Judge when fish are really on feed and then try to gauge just how many there are in the shoal, and what size they may run to. You can then groundbait accordingly.

The exception to the little-and-often rule is when you fish for bream and, to a lesser extent, barbel. For those species it is better to offer a carpet of bait over a small area, possibly for two or three days before you intend to fish. Both species are shy and it is better to make the final heavy groundbaiting some hours before it is intended to fish. After that offer tiny amounts accurately, and disturb the surface of the swim as little as possible. Apart from overfeeding, something hardly likely to happen, the only other crime you can commit with these species is completely to run out of groundbait.

The importance of accurate casting when you groundbait cannot be over emphasised. If you cast by hand, fix a mark against the opposite bank so that each ball is dropped in line with it and at the same distance from your bank. If you use a catapult then note the length of pull that you take with each cast and check the angle at which pouch and handle are held. Practice makes perfect and it is well worth experimenting away from the fishery, perhaps casting loose earth, until you are thoroughly familiar with both your own and your catapult's limitations.

Swim feeders rely on being accurately placed to release and keep groundbait in a small area. But small also applies to the amount of bait that can be fed at one time. Make sure that you pack open-ended feeders so that the bait is released at every cast; over-packing with a stiff mixture or loading with a sloppy one wastes time and effort. Remember that if the swim is too far from your bank to place bait accurately by hand, you can rely on a swim-feeder to do the job. But it will take time.

Bait droppers make sense when you are groundbaiting moving waters, providing that the swim is within easy reach of the rod tip. Its use stops falling particles of groundbait drawing small fish into the area when they are likely to slash excitedly at both baited hook and line. It also stops groundbait from being swept downstream. Don't over-pack the bait pan otherwise it will jam and fail to release the bait. Don't try to cast the dropper beyond rod length and expect the pan to open. Chances are that it will land on its side, preventing the weight from releasing the lid.

If you are fishing in running water make regular checks on the speed of flow. It is no use making the same allowance for the current each time that you throw groundbait in when its speed has increased – possibly by only a small amount, because of the weather, or water control occasioned by a sluice that has been opened or closed upstream.

Speed of current raises the question of groundbaiting when a river is flooded. No matter how stiff the mix or heavy the groundbait, no matter how heavily it may be loaded with stones to make it sink, much of it must be washed downstream and away long before it reaches the bed of a swim. But a river that is coloured and in full flow can be used to the angler's advantage, as we have seen in Chapter 3, dealing with floods.

The Rubby Dubby tin shown in diagram 6 can be cast upstream of a swim with the aid of a long line, the heavy weight at its free end keeping it in place no matter how strong the flood may be. Loaded with bread and bran, or bread and potato, the action of the water will wash it through the large holes drilled in the side of the tin. It takes only minutes to bring ashore, repack and recast, its splash concealed in the rush of rough water.

One last method of groundbaiting remains, and one that requires no preparation or expense on the part of the angler. Raking is normally associated with weed and water clearance, undertaken during the summer months. But besides clearing the water a rake also causes disturbance to the bed and this in turn will release large amounts of natural food. Fish are not slow to find and feed on this, especially during summer months.

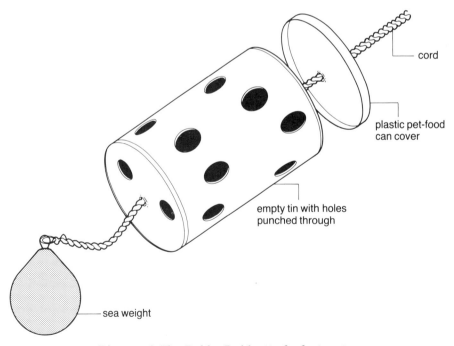

cord

plastic pet-food can cover

empty tin with holes punched through

sea weight

Diagram 6. The Rubby Dubby tin for fast water.

16. Money well spent. This rake has been welded from a strip of reinforcing rod and a heavy garden rake. The curved ends prevent weed from sliding free once uprooted.

A well-made rake is a great asset. Mine is made of concrete reinforcing rod to which is welded a large metal garden rake head. At the other end there is a solid ring, to which is fastened a good length of extra-strong line – see photograph 16. I use it on both still and running water, selecting a likely swim for bream, tench, carp or rudd which I visit on the night before I intend to fish. Cast and retrieved repeatedly over and around an area some 1.5m (5ft) or less in circumference just before the light falls, it never ceases to bring good results at dawn on the day following.

From then on the freshly cleared swim must be fed if you want it to continue to give good sport. On still waters or waters with a mud or silt bed I use a minimum of light-coloured groundbait, plus regular loose offerings of the hookbait that I might be using. When fishing running waters or those with a gravel bed I have found a combination of crushed hempseed together with a few grains of stewed wheat which I also use on the hook to be a successful combination. The combination of rake, hempseed and wheat is especially good when used in clearings made in the middle of weedbeds, fish occasionally browsing in and out of their cover and feeding during the heat of the day.

Chapter 12

NIGHT FISHING WITH MOVEMENT

I am not sure whether the present-day still-water angler who has set himself up to fish through the night could be described as bogged down, or bagged down. Possibly both when you realise that there is no way that he could change his swim or even his tactics should the need arise. Bivouacs big as hotel rooms, camp beds, cooking stoves, the essential transistor plus the usual pile of tackle, food and drink mean that he is as committed as a Scout camp – at least, until daylight arrives.

For many the enthusiasm for camping is greater than their enthusiasm to fish. The need for comfort takes precedence over everything else and although they may have the latest in high-tech tackle, bait and bite indicators they suffer the Feast of the Passover when it comes to counting fish actually out and on the bank.

Night fishing on any water is very hard work. It needs preparation to ensure that everything from the seat down to the last box of bait is working or properly packed. It needs planning to get the gear to the place where it has been decided to fish. And it needs a clear brain, devoid of preconceived ideas of just how and where one is going to put the bait if all that work is going to come together and show rewards. And nowhere can that be more true that when the angler is going to night fish on a river or a water that has movement.

Moving water is never easy to fish during daylight hours. In the dark when one is reduced to relying on a sense of direction and touch it can be nearly impossible. But not quite. For those in the know, who are prepared to experiment and work hard once the sun has gone down, it can be not only rewarding but pleasurable.

You never completely know a swim or the area that surrounds it. If you don't believe this make a sketch map and description of the one you fished most last season and then go back and compare it against your plan. Ten to one there will be at least two important details you have missed, things that could or would make life either difficult or impossible. Bad enough in daylight; possibly tragic if forgotten or overlooked when fishing at night.

It pays to plan in advance before you fish, and that means being prepared to move and fish not just one, but perhaps two or more swims during the course of the night. Often the swim you first settled for will prove a dud. Fish can be difficult to find at night, especially on nights when there is a drop in temperature that so often heralds rain. Rather than sit and doze, be in a position to get up and move to a fresh swim where there might be interest.

If you can, visit the swims a day or so in advance to take stock of surroundings and snags. Be prepared to clear them of excessive weed and to tidy the banks where you are going to be sitting. Last, but by no means least, fix a direction finder in place before you leave.

A direction finder is a small beacon set out on the bank opposite to you which you can see and against which you can cast during darkness. It need be nothing elaborate or even large, and often a piece of silver paper pasted to a board which has been spiked into the ground will work admirably. On smaller waters nothing is more easily seen than a Betanyte light set high enough to be visible over bankside herbage. Remember that your finder, whatever form it takes, should be set upstream of where you want your bait to settle, which means making allowance for the current. If the current has increased on the night that you fish be prepared to go and move it further upstream.

So much for fixing the direction of cast. Now what about the length of cast, the distance you want to reach from your bank every time that you swing the bait out? A difficult problem for which there is no certain solution. Many anglers fix a torch or similar light so that it shines across the water towards the opposite bank. Then either the float, or the splash made by leger weight and bait, can be seen as they hit the water. As a system it works, but it can be tremendously counter productive.

Light actually shining on the water can be an attraction for some fish – mullet for instance, as we have seen in Chapter 8. For many coarse fish the reverse applies and it merely serves to put them well down, unless there is a moon, in which case the light might not be necessary. Some anglers overcome this problem by knotting a piece of nylon on the line leading from the reel at around the same distance as the swim they want to fish lies from the bank. In practice all that is needed should be a swing in the right direction and a slight overcast, so that the bait extends beyond the swim itself. One then reels in until the knot is felt between the fingers and the job is done.

The trouble with this apparently foolproof system is that should you cast short you continue winding in for a long time until there is a sudden and almighty bang as either weights, float or both hit the top ring of the rod. And in the dark the tangle of line around the rod tip will be nearly impossible to free. With practice and some good night vision you will get both the 'feel' and sight of where the bait lands, together with a sixth sense as to just how much force must go into the cast when it is made.

17. The needle and foil method of bite detection. Excellent and sensitive, but trying to find foil strips after each bite can be a time waste at night.

The 'feel', a natural ability to reach for and cope with items that are needed when you are fishing even on the darkest night is one that develops. It is as well to help things on their way by placing items that are normally left outside any light ring that you might want to use in exactly the same place each time it is finished with.

Throughout one long summer I listened carefully for the alarms fitted to various bite detectors that anglers were using when they fished at night. I wasn't listening for the tone or volume, nor was I interested in the strength of their flashing lights. Instead I was interested in studying just how long it took before the angler reached for his rod and switched it off. The answer came to me long before the end of the season and all too clearly. In every case it was far too long.

Somehow a belief in the invincibility of bite detectors of all makes and sizes has crept into angling. There is no doubt that it is greatly to the detriment of the sport. No matter how delicate they may be, how fool-proof they are claimed to be or how carefully they have been set and adjusted, they all at some time or another let you down. Either they fail to detect a bite or they register one that is not taking place. And when you are fishing running water the all-to-frequent non-bite that is given when tackle suddenly lurches forward or is brushed by debris moving downstream can rapidly lead to a downturn of enthusiasm. It cries wolf too often and eventually bites are part-ignored.

By examining and then experimenting with every method, thought and even suggestion on bite detection that I have come across I finally reached the conclusion that there are only two systems worth considering – especially where fishing on running waters is concerned. They are the Betanyte for float work, and the dough bobbin system where legering is employed. The tiny tritium-powdered Betanyte light tip gives out a good, steady glow that doesn't waver. It is as good as anything else on the market providing that it is viewed against a dark background, where movement of any sort can be seen. Where there is no good background or object against which the position of the float can be checked it is possible for a fish to make a slow take without it being realised. Naturally the fish that does that is bound to be a bootlace eel!

Before I adopted the dough bobbin set-up I experimented and nearly took to the needle and foil system of bite indicating. Photograph 17 shows it, a simple set-up where a fish will lift the line against the weight of the foil. I abandoned it because after each strike it took time and disturbance to find the foil which had been thrown from the line. A small item I admit, but important when you are trying to keep noise and light away from the water.

Dough bobbins need a light source against which they can be seen. When torches became the norm in night fishing I changed over to one that gave a flat light at my feet and tried to get used to it. Within a season I had changed back to a gas-fired storm lamp heavily shaded despite the fact that it was a nuisance to carry.

The reason for the change was a softness of light that did not destroy night vision completely. With the torch I was blind beyond my feet; with the storm light I can see, if only in outline, beyond my immediate surroundings. Don't get me wrong, I'm not one of your steam-driven anglers and I do use a torch, but only when a fish is hooked. It is one of the smaller Solitaire models capable of having the beam trained into a spot, which I hold in my mouth. Anything bigger, especially models which have to be strapped to the head, should be confined to night shooting at rabbits.

The beauty of using dough bobbins is that they indicate not just the slightest movement that a fish may make, but also give some indication of what they might be doing. The ultra-slow gentle lift can be spotted and diagnosed as probably coming from an obstruction, possibly a leaf or twig that is held against the line in the current. The drop of a weight, sudden tiny twitches that return the bobbin to its original position, can be seen, recognised and dealt with. With electronic detectors of any sort much can take place before it is signalled, and once it has been signalled then the chance to diagnose what caused it has disappeared.

I have seen some anglers use swingtips, quivertips or a dough bobbin pinched on line at the rod tip as a method of bite detecting when they leger. Some use a target board against which a light is directed, allowing clear vision of the tip indicator that is being used. They work, though it must be said that in the case of the dough indicator it means the angler must constantly be getting up from his seat to fix it. I prefer the butt-indicating bobbin system. Not only can I use it without getting out of my seat, but I can also shelter and protect it from movement when there is a strong wind.

Weather can play strange tricks at night. It takes very little rain to make a bank slippery, and only a little wind to cause enough water disturbance that will hide the depth at the edge. This means that when you are going to land a fish from a high bank be sure that you really know just what the ground at the landing place is like. More than one angler has taken an early bath because in his enthusiasm he strode manfully on to what he thought was a safe footing. Be prepared by knowing that small piece of water in front of you as well as you have got to know the swim that you are fishing.

Chapter 13
SLUG IT TO 'EM

You don't qualify as a paid-up, fully-fledged, died-in-the-wool angler unless you have a few hang-ups. We've all got them and they mostly centre around carrying good-luck charms or performing good-luck rites at the water side. Some of the more mentionable (and stupid) include not pulling the landing net together until the first fish is hooked, then promptly losing it because the net wasn't ready, or wearing ridiculous head gear more suited to the member's enclosure at Ascot than a river bank.

But when hang-ups become obsessions, and tranquilliser-sized obsessions at that, things are going too far. Two are in special vogue at the moment, the first centring on baits. It would seem that regardless of the size or type of rod or rig being used, or the species being fished for, only the tiniest of baits may be put on to the hook. And by tiny I mean small enough to fit a pygmy's blow-pipe.

The second concerns weed. Whether it is surface growing or spread under-water, part filling or merely flanking the angler's swim, it will be regarded and treated in much the same way as a minefield in the Red Sea. To which the thinking angler must ask — why?

I am convinced that both obsessions have arrived as a spin-off from match fishing. Take that matter of tiny baits. Once the whistle blows at the start of a competition pressure will be on to catch fish in quantity rather than fish of quality. No matter how small the fish it must be hooked, and as Murphy's Law states that there will be more small than big fish in a swim a tiny bait that can be mouthed in one gulp would seem the most sensible to put on offer. Not only that, but there will be little fear of that tiny bait disturbing fish as it hits the water or sinks into the swim.

The same reasoning applies to the obsession against weed. Tiny baits demand tiny hooks which in turn require a fine, low breaking-strain line. Put that sort of rig close to weed and there is bound to be a time-consuming, fish-frightening break at some time.

This should not be allowed to happen while a competition is being fished. But the 'small and fine are beautiful' syndrome seems to have spilled into everyday angling, spoiling the chances of many would-be all-rounders from getting into the real sport of catching big fish consistently.

18. Old satchel mouth himself! There is little point in using a tiny hook and a tiny bait when a chub's mouth of this size is waiting to be filled.

Let's start by getting one or two things clear. First of all, fish are used to hearing splash and feeling vibration when objects hit the water. Some natural and commonplace occurrences are banks that collapse and branches from trees that break and fall in. But more important from the angler's point of view is that fish actually rely heavily on disturbance and noise to indicate that food has arrived. Items such as seeds, fruits, insects and their larvae together with small mammals that fall or are dislodged into the water are just a few instances.

Today, surface disturbance in angling has advanced one stage further. Fish have become conditioned into looking for food, and feeding, as the result of the angler's groundbaiting tactics. Seed baits and maggots broadcast over the surface, large balls of cereal baits depth-charged into a small area, the pike angler's deadbait hitting the water all both attract fish from a distance and stimulate an immediate feeding cycle. This kills off that 'let's keep it small when we fish' idea.

Now, weed. Fish love weed. They are born in it, brought up in it, eat it, rely on it for shelter from the elements and for protection from their natural enemies. They may occasionally be drawn out and away from it by the skill of an angler who groundbaits carefully, but by and large they know a good thing when in on it, so they stay put. And that includes the bigger and better fish.

Which means that a big bait, cast into and worked through weedbeds with a hefty splash, stands an equal chance of catching a fish as a small one does. And there is a vastly increased chance that the big bait will pull a big fish.

There are few big baits that can withstand that sort of work without coming adrift from the hook. Not surprisingly the best of those available are all naturals. Big lobworms come to mind, pieces of swan mussel, small crayfish (where they can be obtained), and the list is about complete. Except for the most important one: the common or garden slug.

Slug fishing is in a league of its own, needing precious little in the way of complicated tackle. It has long been established as a deadly bait for chub, taking fish out of near-impossible places. But it is not a style for the squeamish, or for those who are lazy.

First there is the task of finding slugs, no easy job during hot summer months when most have gone to ground. Then, providing they have been correctly kept, they need to be mounted on to the hook, a squelch-producing trauma if not done properly. But take it from me the suicidal response from fish of all species, and especially big chub to whom an accurately cast slug has been freelined, must be seen to be believed.

Rivers produce the best returns. Not fast-flowing waters that whip across barren stone and rock strewn bottoms, but those that are slow flowing, with weed-supporting stretches which keep the main current easing along the centre of the stream, the gravel bed running at an even depth with only an occasional deep hole.

There are dozens like them throughout the Midlands and South of England each of them well laced, often choked with rush and reedmace beds together with a supporting cast of overhanging trees and bushes that lean well over the water. Size is not important, though it will be more difficult to get a rod on to some small streams where the whole area has grown together to form an arch. But there is nothing that can compete against an angler armed with water craft, determination and stealth.

If you are one of the died-in-the-wool tackle box, bait-stand, keepnet and groundbait brigade forget any ideas you may have of slug fishing. Slugging demands that the angler be entirely mobile, prepared to carry whatever he needs fastened to or hanging from his body, leaving both hands free for rod, landing net and fish.

With this style the best and safest way to fish is to get in with them, which means that where the river bed is firm and capable of supporting the angler's weight then it is a wading job, with the angler working upstream and casting ahead, clear of bankside vegetation.

It is rough work scrambling through and around weed beds and those who practise the sport on a regular basis take care to wear heavy industrial-type waders. The thin green variety associated with the game fishing brigade is no match for this work, and often tear the first time they make contact with an underwater obstruction.

Faced with a water where you can't wade then it's a question of scrabble and creep along the banks, keeping below the skyline and looking for a place to get the bait in the water. During dry weather trainers make excellent footwear for this type of work. But cold and damp conditions demand something better and for my money waders are the safest and driest bet.

For comfort a fly-fishing type waistcoat provided with half a dozen or so pockets will hold spare hooks and a disgorger, together with a large towel (essential for cleaning the hands after a slug has been mounted on the hook), a sensibly sized pair of scissors for line repairs, and a spring balance.

Whether you wade or bank fish you will need the best pair of polarising glasses you can afford if you are to get the most from the day. There are many cheap pairs on the market, many of which do little to rest the eyes from glare, or worse, fail to cut refraction to allow a view into the water in front of you. Pay a good price for a known brand and at the same time purchase either a sun shade, or a cap with an extra-wide brim. Sun kept from the front of the glasses will help your underwater vision considerably.

Equally important but considerably cheaper will be the bait carrier you will need in which to carry some 30 or so slugs – the minimum needed for a reasonable day. Ideally one of the white plastic buckets with lid and handle, frequently used by the D.I.Y. trade to market filler and tile grouting should be found. It must be clean, have holes pierced in its lid and be capable of being strapped to your belt, carried on one hip, ready at hand level.

The all-important rod, reel and landing net will be already possessed by the majority. My choice is for a 0.7kg (1½lb) T.C. rod some 3.3m (11ft) long, a 1.8kg (4lb) monofiliment line and a closed-face fixed-spool reel. My justification for selecting a closed-face reel is that it stops odd loops of line from hanging down and catching on clothing or vegetation.

Finally, there is the choice of landing net. I learned slugging from Charlie Landells, the chub fishing ace, and adopted his choice of a collapsing shoulder-slung landing net as being the best possible. Since then I have revised my thoughts, and now use the traditional net with long, firm handle that acts as a wading staff. It can be driven into the ground beside me when I am fishing, ready if required.

It is not over-dramatising to say that it needs guts to wade out into a well-weeded river, especially one not fished before. It's a question of hurry slowly, work upstream, take one step at a time and test the bed before shifting weight. But practice brings confidence, and once that state is reached the brain can concentrate on the finer arts that bring success.

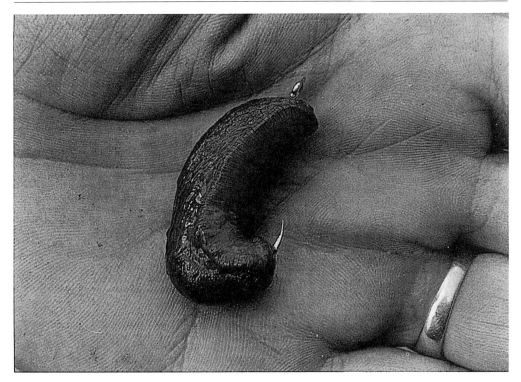

19. Properly mounted a slug will fish through weedbeds without snagging, yet hook properly when it is taken.

This is one style unaffected by bright sunlight, in fact, the brighter the light the better the results provided fish aren't frightened. Casting upstream helps to prevent that, and also means that should any shadow from your body land across the water, it will be too far below the fish to be seen. But slugging can be miserable work in strong wind and rain, both of which affect the accuracy of a cast and promote line cling to the rod itself.

Slugs should be mounted onto a size 4 or 6 hook. Try to buy those with the longest shank possible; a search through the sea fishing section of a tackle shop will provide the best. Slip the point of the hook into the back of the slug near one end, feed it along the shank and bring the point out at the other end. The bait should fit completely along the hook, without hanging down or bunching onto the bend. Provided this is done, there will be little chance of the hook catching in weed beds or coming adrift during the cast. (See photograph 19)

Aim for clumps of thin-stemmed weed that show above the surface, and let the bait dive-bomb into them. Hand-tighten the line immediately and be prepared for an instant and violent take. If a chub is hungry then it will mean business, so much so that there will be little or no need to strike. But once that hook goes home into old 'shovel-mouth' be prepared for fireworks.

If there is no immediate response, try working the bait back towards you, pulling slowly, allowing it to sink and draw by raising and lowering the rod tip. Again, you will be left in no doubt when a fish takes.

Don't stand any nonsense, take charge and bully the chub from the word go. There may be a chance that you will get a break, but once you let a hefty fish get its head, it will have the line wound into the weed and break free in a flash. Better go down fighting than be left with a stranded fish!

There are two cautions that go with the style. One is to avoid casting close to tree roots. Quite apart from your getting tangles on the cast, a hooked chub that reaches underwater roots is as good as free. Remember also that fish are not so fast at taking the bait when the light is poor, so allow more time to work the bait, and be prepared to make repeat casts if the first offer is ignored.

So much for the excitement and uncertainty of the sport. Now for the nasties: slugs, catching and keeping them. Of the 20 or so species found in this country, only three are of any real use to the angler, the Red, Great Grey and the Black. Mostly you can find them following wet weather in garden borders and vegetable patches, around compost heaps and under stones, rockeries, etc. Once the weather turns hot and dry they will disappear.

Three options face the angler when this happens. One is to set traps for them such as a marrow cut length-wise and opened, old cabbage stumps and unwanted cabbage leaves placed in well-watered areas of long grass at the foot of hedges and flower beds. The second, more difficult and time-consuming method is to keep and breed your own stock.

An aquarium is the best vessel to keep and breed in, one with a close-fitting lid, planted with around 15cm (6in) of soil on to which slats of wood or bark fibre are placed. A few big, rough stones or small flowerpots set on their sides will provide cover, and a quantity of household waste, potato peelings, cabbage leaves, etc. will complete the living quarters.

Keeping the aquarium covered will seal moisture in, an important need but one that can, when there are a large number of inhabitants, cause problems. Tilting will draw moisture to one end where it can be syphoned off. Search regularly for dead inhabitants, add fresh stock as often as you can, and you should have supply enough for the season.

The third and final option comes into its own during severe drought conditions. Try using freshwater or garden snails as bait, as big as possible, with the hard shell crushed before being mounted onto the hook. And in utter desperation, use whelks purchased from your local fishmonger. Expensive to a point, but eased from their shell and mounted on the hook, they can often bring excellent sport.

Chapter 14

KEEPING AFLOAT

It's another fine mess we've got ourselves into with this float business. There was a time when you could guarantee that any angler you met on the bank would have about six or so floats, the remainder of his tackle box being taken up with sandwiches. Today that box is likely to be packed with floats in such numbers and sizes that nothing other than a packet of Polo mints could be squeezed in.

Why? Don't ask the angler. He won't have a clue. In the majority of cases he is either blindly following the lead given by his friends or club members and keeping up with what they take with them, or he is genuinely trying to be prepared for any and every angling situation and species of fish that he might want to fish for.

Why do we need a float at all? Very often we don't and most anglers are now well aware that if a float can be avoided, it should be. But when it *is* required it is needed for several valid reasons. First to control the bait, which means holding it at a predetermined depth, keeping it on the move and away from the bottom where it might get snagged. It is also used for moving a bait via the wind or current into an area normally impossible to reach, perhaps banks overgrown with treees.

We may need a float to indicate attention from a fish when it takes or even mouths the bait, regardless of how gentle or slow this might be. This is an important detail and one we are all aware of, though often not consciously so. Coupled with this is the possibility that the movement of the float can also give a clue to the species of fish or the manner in which it has got hold of the bait. It is also possible to gauge some idea of its size, more especially if it is something small.

Finally, the float is capable of giving some indication of where a fish is and the direction in which it is travelling after it has been hooked and during the time that it is being played, including the depth at which it is moving as well as its speed.

I have met anglers who are emphatic in their belief that the float is also needed to add weight to the line which will help cast a bait – especially a light one. That is rubbish. Weight is responsible for pulling line through the rod rings for the duration of a cast. If anything, a float is counter-productive, often 'kiting' on the

20. How many floats are needed – especially floats of one particular type? There seem to be a few that are duplicated in this random selection.

wind and reducing accuracy, especially when long casts are attempted. There are many other anglers who insist that a float is needed to provide a focus point, something to concentrate on. I would not disagree with this, as long as the other reasons that have been outlined are remembered.

So those are some of the reasons for using a float. But that begs a whole galaxy of questions such as what types of float should be used, which are the best ones, and how many – or how few – should actually be carried?

The type of float that should be used must be governed by the type of water that is being fished and, to a lesser extent, the species of fish that the angler is trying to catch. For years there was an angling maxim which said that the bigger the water you were fishing, the bigger the float. And in days when a big float was a swan's quill about 0.3m (1ft) long, that probably meant that a fair number of bites were not even recognised. We have progressed since then and we now know that the float may have to be big on a big water, but it should also be sensitive.

93

Sensitivity is influenced by three factors: the material from which the float is made, the way that it is shotted down into the water, and its size (circumference) at the point where it leaves the surface – the actual piece that you look at, or should look at, all the time. But the vast majority of floats that are made will only be sensitive when they are used on a particular type of water. And as, in general terms, types of water fall into four main headings – fast, slow, big and small – the choice of which one to use and, even more important, how many to carry should be easy. At this point it is as well that we discuss some of the waters and floats that will suit them.

Waters which are big, fast-flowing and rough will need a float that will carry a bait well down in the water over long distances. The Avon-type float was designed to meet the requirements of long trotting. Originally made from balsa, some recent designs on the market have largely superseded them. The new Avon floats are moulded from clear plastic that helps to reduce their appearance to fish in gin-clear water. Broad shouldered, the top of the float is short and thin, keeping wind resistance to the minimum and drawing a balance between visibility and sensitivity.

Large still-waters often demand long casts to reach fish, and this in turn will call for a float big enough to support the weight added to the line. But the float

21. Floats for special occasions. These three are indispensable when fishing in weirpools.

must be ultra sensitive, able to record the slightest touch made by a fish and visible when anchored in rough, wind-swept waters. The fat-bodied waggler is possibly the best solution, its body built onto the last third of a stick and suspended well down below the surface. It can carry a lot of weight and remain steady, the thin stem visible in all but the worst storm.

If the weather reaches those proportions then a windbeater top, a blob built onto the top of the float well above the water, will make it visible for a considerable distance. If there is any fault with the waggler float, including the many sub-species that it has spawned, it is the fact that many anglers use them through force of habit to the exclusion of anything else.

So much for the long-distance, heavyweight float. Now what about those run-of-the-mill fisheries, both still and running waters, where the angler will want to put and keep a bait within easy casting distance of the bank? If you believe what you see on the water there are hundreds of floats that could or should be used. Balsa floats, sticks, wagglers fat and thin, loaded floats, quills – all are mounted to the line in profusion. But what is really needed?

The answer must be the smallest float possible which is sensitive to the water conditions, able to control the bait and unlikely to be seen by fish below the surface. Not only that, but once it is selected it should be capable of remaining in use throughout the day unless some dire emergency in the weather occurs. The modern fad for changing floats every hour or so because the one in use doesn't suit the mood, isn't sitting correctly on the water or, as I have heard anglers say 'finding fish' (whatever that may mean), is complete rubbish. Of course adjustments are needed when you fish with a float, but they should be to its position on the line or to the position of the weights below it.

There are specialist floats that come into their own when the angler is fishing on a difficult water, and he should not be without them. One that immediately comes to mind is the self-cocking float that allows a bait to be presented on the drop, especially useful when rudd, dace or roach are feeding in the mid or upper sections of a swim. In an emergency one can always be made by looping a length of nylon through the end ring of a stick float and fastening lead-substitute shot to it in much the same way as for the swan shot leger.

Another essential float worth carrying at all times is the slider. The need to fish over a really deep hole can always arise, and this is the sure way of dealing with it. But there are sliders and sliders. Many are made with the end and top ring far too close to the body. Make sure you get a float where they stand well proud, allowing the line to run freely without clinging or rubbing against the body of the float itself.

If there is one section of the angling fraternity that has really got its act together where floats are concerned it must be the pike fishermen. You can get pike floats long and thin, or short and round, and either will work depending on the weather that you may encounter. Of course the real beauty lies in the fact that they are designed so that you can thread the line through the body of the float itself, adjusting for depth by way of a stop knot on the line. One day I hope that some of the bigger floats for general coarse fishing will work on the same principle.

Floats for use with the roachpole are in a class of their own. Yet in many cases it is possible to freeline with a roachpole and do away with the float altogether. The beauty of the pole float is that it is stored ready-mounted on line and hook, which stops the bother of shotting up at the waterside.

So how many floats are really needed to cover the situation you are likely to meet when you fish? Just how many should be in that tackle box, specialist fishing such as pike and pole work apart? My choice is two different-sized wagglers and two different-sizes of Avon trotters to cover the big waters. Certainly a self-cocking float, and I would not be without a slider in two sizes at any time.

After that? Well as far as I am concerned a couple of medium-sized sticks and a brace of very thin wagglers are useful. But they are nowhere near as useful as a couple of good, long lengths of peacock quill that can be cut to make the actual size of float that you require when you decide on a swim, mounted to the line either by one or both ends with rubber float caps. Their natural white tops are one of the most useful colours for a float, visible against the vast majority of backgrounds. Where white is not visible a red or black waterproof felt marker can provide one that is acceptable in seconds.

Chapter 15

SUMMER SPINNING

There was a time when summer spinning was considered neither sporting nor practical. Pike fishing in the summer was definitely against all the self-inflicted rules of angling for reasons that largely centred around late spawning times, unfit fish ('gravid' was the favourite term), a need for frost to make the brutes feed and so on. As for spinning, there was little sense in it. If the fish were interested then the spinners would definitely be unable to cope with weed growth and shallow water. Even today during summer months there is hesitation on the part of some anglers to take a spinning rod to predators. The message still circulates that weed in the water will be more likely to take a bait than a fish.

I suppose that the fear of tackle loss is a reasonable one in today's financial climate. Spinners are not cheap, line is positively dear, and add to those major items such small but significant details as swivels, leads and traces and the cost of a good, let alone a really bad day out, could soon mount up.

But as I commented earlier in this book nothing in angling is completely cut and dried. There are waters and waters, just as there are spinners and spinners. The secret is in knowing those waters which should be left well alone and knowing spinners that shouldn't be allowed close to the end of a line. It's the same old story, a little negative thinking can bring some very positive results.

Let's start by acknowledging that weed need not completely obstruct a waterway. There will be gaps where it does not grow either because of the current or because there is insufficient sunlight reaching a particular area for it to prosper. Even where there is a good head of weed growing in a water it is quite possible that it won't reach to the surface, and that there can be clear water between it and the surface itself.

So all is not doom and gloom and there can be clear areas in both still and running water where a spinner can be worked without worry. Some of them may be small, but there are ways and means of getting the most out of even the smallest. Now we have dealt with the where, let's consider how.

The problem that rears its ugly head in summer spinning is not the spinner itself. It is the treble that trails behind it – and note that 'treble' was used in the singular. As a general rule it will pay to remove one hook from the body of a spinner that carries two. Where this cannot be done and the spinner is expensive or a 'one-off' that is impossible to replace it is better to leave it in the tackle box.

There have been spinners on the market over the years that were advertised as having snag-proof hooks. That usually meant they had been fitted with some sort of spring clip – rather like that fitted to a dog's lead – that was supposed to stop weed from tangling. Some were supplied with two large single hooks fastened to a single split ring both facing inwards, the idea being that each point would be hidden behind the bend of the other hook.

In Barrie Rickards's collection which he brought back from Russia I saw a non-snag hook where the spinner was in two halves, with the hooks protected by them until a fish took hold. When that happened the body was compressed and two single hooks were forced out and into the mouth of the fish. Both it and all the other so-called snag-free hooks and hook-spinner combinations which I have outlined could not be regarded as infallible.

So what is? A single hook mounted on its own at the end of a spinner is safer and more likely to remain uncluttered than a big treble. Trebles smaller in size than the body of the spinner they are mounted to are also safer. Yes, there is a school of thought which insists that the width across the gape of the combined treble should be equal to, or greater than, the width of the body. Without that essential measurement it is held as being unlikely that a fish could be hooked. They are right to a certain extent. But as a compromise the smaller size is not such a bad deal. At least the spinner should last long enough to attract a fish.

One extra-safe way of preventing a lure being snagged is to cover the hooks altogether. That idea is not as daft as it may seem. Cover the treble with breadpaste of some kind, made a little on the stiff side, and there is protection enough to deal with all but the thickest and toughest weed beds. When the take occurs the paste will be thrown or worked clear. There are other forms of padding that can protect trebles. Small cubes of cheese are one, but better are worms, common or garden varieties, several secured to each hook. They not only provide protection but add attraction, as do small sandeels when they can be obtained.

Our American cousins are well into the anti-snag business. One of the lures that they produce is an excellent weed fisher called the Bomber Bushwacker. It is an odd construction of leaf spinner mounted to one end of an angled piece of wire with hooks (two large singles mounted one on the other) plus a frilled piece of plastic mounted around them and secured to the other end of the wire. The whole thing has a distinctly lop-sided look on dry land, but in practice the lure works well. Weed will strike against the wire during a retrieve and trip everything sideways frequently preventing a tangle, while the plastic frill that looks like a psychedelic octopus serves to give the hook some added protection.

But all baits need not be big, even when the biggest pike needs to be attracted

OPPOSITE

22. A selection of spinners suitable for summer spinning – after the hooks have been replaced with smaller ones, less than the width of the body. Second from the left is the Bomber Bushwacker.

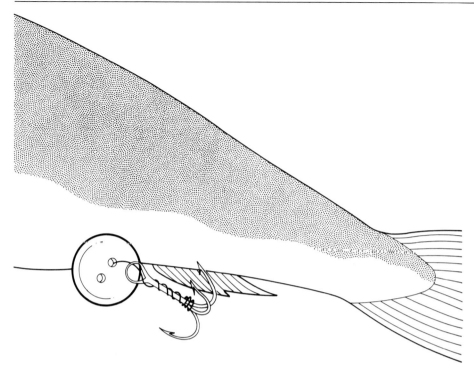

Diagram 7. The button stop that prevents the treble being drawn into a deadbait.

and hooked. There are plenty of small lures on the market that will skim above the tops of weeds, seek and work out the layer of water between weed and surface, and with the addition of a lead substitute swan shot or two to the line, work sink-and-draw through a big or deep hole. Fly spoons, tiny leaf spinners and fly/spinner crosses are but a few. It is worth noting that some of the fly/spinner crosses have feathers fastened to the shank of the hook which serves as some form of hook protection against weed.

When weed really makes a takeover, and when the heat of summer drops water levels so much that large areas of waterweed are exposed to lie on the surface, that is the time to stop spinning with the artificial and to use a deadbait. Some of the biggest specimens in the big fish lists are taken by this method, which does not demand that the bait itself has actually to be revolved in the same way that is expected of an artificial.

Spinning where a deadbait is concerned includes a slow, complete revolution, wobbling either from side to side or up and down and, naturally, the sink-and-draw style. Baits do not need to be long, the best in my experience being small roach, dace or bleak, not more than 10–13cm (4–5in) at the most, mounted by having the line threaded through the body from vent to mouth with the aid of a baiting needle. A single large treble should be brought up against the vent and prevented from drawing into the body by the aid of a button (see diagram 7).

Cast straight out and then retrieved slowly this simple rig will produce a wobble to the bait, its speed equal to the speed of the retrieve given by the angler. Where a spin is required an ordinary snap tackle should be used, taking care to curve the body slightly between tail and head treble. The degree of spin will vary with the amount of curve given to the bait. Weight is not normally required when spinning with a deadbait. If the bait is required to work deep, just let it take its time to sink. You are in no rush, there is all day to fish in, and the chances are that the bait will be taken as it sinks naturally from sight.

Summer spinning can pay a dividend of its own when it is employed along stretches of water that are regularly occupied by the match fishermen. Their constant groundbaiting serves to collect large shoals of fry that pike, perch and chub will run through with open mouths, grabbing at what they can. Strong though the temptation may be it is better to wait until the match is over before spinning among the pegs. If the fish are uninterested for some reason, it is worth the effort of baiting one or two swims up with a little breadcrumb groundbait, waiting until fish assemble, or a strike by a predator is seen, before spinning through them.

One of the big weed problems mentioned elsewhere is duckweed. Great, long banks of it will completely cover small, slow rivers and lakes that are open to the heat of the sun to any great extent. The immediate reaction is to leave such stretches alone. But when you stop and apply a little extra thought it will be realised that fish must still be there, under the weed. There is nowhere else for them to go, and they still need to feed. Spin as you would for a normal clear water and take benefit from a bonus. In most cases, the thick blanket of surface weed will have smothered and killed rooted weed growing beneath it.

When you are looking for big problems the small ones tend to get overlooked, and that can be very dangerous. One of the effects of spinning through weed will be to pack pieces of it into the swivels that are used, jamming them solid and preventing them from turning. Check them at regular intervals through the day and replace those that don't work. You can clear and clean them when you get home.

If you are weeded when you fish in running water then don't forget the otter (no relation to the poacher's otter board), that round plastic disc that can be fastened onto the line and allowed to slide down it to the spinner. With some help from the current even an impossible snagging can result in a happy release.

Chapter 16

DIFFERENT BAITS, BETTER FISH

'It's fished out!' How many times have you heard that said about a water? And how many times have you believed it, accepting the statement without further thought? Yet when you think about it, it is practically impossible to fish a water out. The fish are not taken away by anglers, nor has the water been netted or drained. What is really meant is not that the water is fished out, but that fish in the water have become wary of the angler and his antics, especially those which centre around the baits that he uses.

We frequently regard fish as 'stupid', not 'deliberately' perhaps but simply through force of 'habit'. And the biggest habit, the one that many anglers never break, is the one that lets them rely on one particular bait to the exclusion of all others when they visit certain fisheries. Because of previous successes, the winning weights in club matches, or the knowledge that big fish taken from that particular water have all been achieved through the use of, say bread, then it is immediately used to the exclusion of all other baits, day in and day out, for year after year.

Never once will it occur to anglers that fish may unconsciously tire of the same bait or, more important still, that they will become 'educated' to the fact that if they continue to feed on whatever it is that is repeatedly offered, there is every chance they will be caught. If you think that is a tall story then just stop and think of a stretch of water – especially a still water – heavily match-fished every weekend and perhaps during several weekdays throughout a season.

A high proportion of fish in all sizes will certainly be caught at least once, and some several times over. In fact the harder the water is fished the greater their chance of being caught increases. No wonder that over a period of time fish will appear to have become scarce or even completely absent from the water and that there are cries for the water to be re-stocked. But the fish are not missing – they just will not approach the angler's hook. Further evidence? Then think about the dropped-bait syndrome that has sprung up on well-fished pike waters. It was once practically unknown. Now, through anglers constantly fishing and ground-baiting with deadbaits, fish are suspicious of baits lying on the bottom.

But what new bait could be used on a popular and established fishery? What would appeal to fish already bombarded with food that would break the vice of repetition? Human instinct suggests something natural, perhaps an insect or vertebrate which is so attractive either by colour or action that fish will accept it without hesitation.

My experience supports that. It has also proved that a new bait on a water does not need to be natural in the accepted sense. In fact the reverse often applies, a bait with which fish could never naturally come into contact proving successful. That leaves the field wide open to anglers with some imagination and patience.

One bait which falls into that category and can liven up a fished-out water is the crayfish. Though quite widespread in many of our rivers and canals across the country the crayfish is often unknown to anglers. This is not so surprising when you understand that those small, dark brown freshwater 'lobsters' which may grow to a length of 13cm (5in) (and which can give a pretty sharp nip from their claws) are largely nocturnal, living in holes under the banks.

The nocturnal tag would suggest that this should be a bait to be fished only at night, when fish would find them out and about. In fact the reverse is true, and a small crayfish or even part of a cray will be taken at any time. Fish that will willingly accept them include chub, barbel, pike and perch, the degree of interest that they show largely depending on the way that the bait is fished.

Catching crayfish is nearly as much fun as fishing with them. A drop-net operated at night is the perfect trap, baited with meat or fish. Many anglers insist that the bait should be 'ripe'. My experience shows the reverse, and I get my best results when I use a piece of fresh kipper. Once caught, crayfish can be kept in wet weed for immediate use, or stored in a pond or large bucket for use in the future.

Kill them by crushing the head with a pair of pliers. Some prefer boiling them before use, which turns them dark red, a colour said to represent a cray that is in the process of casting its shell, an added attraction to fish. The majority, myself included, prefer to use either a small (up to 5cm/2in) whole crayfish or the tail end of one broken free from the head end of the body and mounted on a suitably sized hook.

Whole or large pieces (tails) of crayfish are best freelined. They will hold well onto a single hook threaded through one of the tail segments, and can be cast in the same way as a spinner or plug before being made to work close to bank sides, near weedbeds and around obstructions. Smaller crayfish or pieces used as bait are best fished with the aid of a float. In fact where you would fish a slug is the place to put a crayfish. Though you usually associate running water with cray fishing it is possible to use them where there is little or no current, such as canals. On that type of fishery they are best legered.

There is a substitute for the crayfish which brings results equal to, and in some cases better than, fishing with the real thing. Prawns from the fishmonger bear a resemblance when they are prepared by having the head removed together

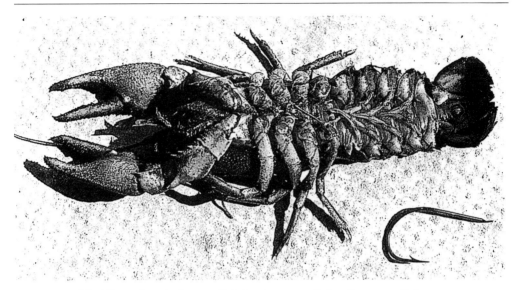

23. The tail end of a crayfish is strong medicine for many fish.

with some of the shell covering along the back. Leave the tail and legs in place, then mount and fish in exactly the same way as described for the crayfish. Heads, scales and a few broken-up prawns thrown into the swim as a free offering help to bring better results.

Another bait that can attract good fish, specimens even, on overfished waters is the swan mussel. It has often been recommended as a tench bait, but my experience shows that several other species will fall for it, especially big eels. Many anglers say that they cannot get on with mussels despite waiting long hours and taking great time and trouble to present this bait correctly. I suffered a horrendous series of blanks until I sat down and gave some thought to just how fish of any species could get at the meat inside the shells of a mussel.

To understand that you must first learn a little about them. Mussels are bivalve molluscs which can be found in mud on the bottom of either lakes, ponds or slower-flowing rivers. They tend to live in colonies in fairly shallow water, allowing a number to be gathered easily if you wade out and feel across the bottom for them, or alternatively work with a rake and drag them to the water's edge.

In their natural state the two shell edges are kept firmly closed by the aid of a leathery ligament or hinge on the top side of the shells. As mussels live by filtering mud and extracting food through a side valve, there is no need for the shell ever to open completely. This means that the only chance that a fish will have to feed on mussel 'meat' will be after its death when muscles have relaxed, the hinge has opened and the insides exposed. There is no doubt that by the time that happened the whole molluscs would be rotten and ripe!

That is the secret in using a mussel as bait. Collect them several days before they are needed and leave them out in the sun exactly as they are without opening them. Given two or three days they can be detected by their smell, and carried at arm's length to the selected swim, together with soap and a towel.

Opening mussels requires some thought – especially if all one's fingers on each hand are to remain intact. Take a knife and slip it through one side opposite to the hinge. Run it round as far as the hinge itself, then take the knife and run it back the other way and this time through the hinge itself. Both halves will come apart. Don't part-open and try to force the two shell halves apart – the muscle of the hinge, even in death, is stronger than you think!

Groundbaiting is vitally important. I make up a normal bread mix to which I add half a dozen or so mussels chopped up into small pieces, adding any fluid that may still be contained between the shells. Finally I crush the shells themselves into tiny pieces and add these to the mix. The pearl-coloured inside pieces show up well against the bottom and help to advertise the presence of the groundbait, which should be cast into a small area of the swim close to mussel beds if that is possible. It is at this point that use of the soap and towel for your hands becomes vital – unless you wish to clear both banks of anglers. But keep the soap away from the water!

24. Both fresh and saltwater mussels, opened and the body removed ready to be mounted on to a hook.

There are enormous increases in results obtained when the groundbait mixing has been done the day before it is intend to fish, leaving the 'juice' and flesh to transfer its smell and taste into the bread. But it needs a strong stomach (and a sound marriage) for this undertaking to be attempted close to the house.

For the hook, select the pink foot from an open mussel, that is the solid piece close to the edge of the shell, remove it and cut it to the size needed before mounting it. (See photograph 24) Legering is the rig most frequently chosen to present the bait in running waters, with a hook in the size 2 to 4 range tied directly to the line. In small, still waters I much prefer to use a fingernail-sized piece of flesh, with the aid of a lift rig and a hook about size 10 to 8, keeping the baited hook well inside the groundbaited area. Remember that it is not always a big bait that takes the biggest fish, especially when you are summer tench fishing.

Where it is difficult to harvest swan mussels, or on water where they appear to be completely absent, it is possible to substitute the saltwater mussel, using it in the same way as I have described for the freshwater variety. During the season they are reasonably cheap which means that a good number can be prepared and mixed for groundbait. They can also be frozen and stored, ready for late autumn or use at the opening of the season.

The widely held theory that the easiest and perhaps the only way to get bait for fishing is by going to the tackle shop with a bait box and buying it means that some of the best natural baits are overlooked and in many instances almost forgotten. One such bait is caddis fly larvae, the protective cases of which are works of art. Built from materials in the area where they live the tiny tubes, open at one end to allow head and front legs to protrude, provide almost perfect camouflage. There is hardly a water in the country from which they are absent, from tiny mountains streams to the dead-looking drains and guts of a marsh.

There are two ways of catching them. One is to rake through weed banks, hauling the greenery up on to the bank and then making a physical search through the leaves and stalks. The other way taught to me as a child is to tie two or three stalks from brassica plants – cabbage or sprouts – together and lower these into water known to contain larvae. The stalks present a fatal attraction and numbers of caddis cases can be lifted after a period of 24 hours.

Don't attempt to carry caddis bait in water. It will quickly become de-oxygenated and kill them. Instead fill a plastic box with water weed, soak it, and place the larvae amongst it, repeating the soaking at regular intervals and storing the box out of the sun. Keep larvae not wanted for fishing in the garden pond which no prudent angler is ever without.

Whichever style you intend to use when you fish the grub, make sure it is presented at its best by mounting it on the finest wire hook you can obtain. I go down to size 18, and after breaking its shell housing apart lightly nick the grub by its tail end taking care not to squash or break it open. Only one groundbait

*25. The comb from a wasp nest that holds the grubs. Once they
have been taken the whole comb together with the outside case
can be pulped for ground and hookbait.*

could possibly be used with such a big, white hookbait and that is the maggot, white, and preferably dropped onto the bed of the swim by the aid of a bait layer.

If you swim the stream then make sure that an extra lead substitute dust shot is nipped on to the trace just above the hook itself. Without it, the larvae will rise up and drift in front of the line, giving fish the chance to mouth and squash without registering a bite. It takes little effort to gather and carry this summer-time bait, which is an absolute killer for roach and tench. They also freeze, and provide a winning bait in winter when you are long trotting and roach and dace are a little bit 'iffy' when they bite.

The final and most deadly bait worth trying on any tired and over-worked fishery will not present itself as a natural item in the water. Every angler will have heard of wasp grubs and their deadly attraction to fish of all sorts, though few will have actually fished with them. The reason for this lack of use stems more from difficulty in finding and then removing wasp nests during the season than from lack of enthusiasm.

Keen as I am on collecting and preparing my own natural baits I gave up collecting wasp nests several seasons ago. The reason came not from the danger of being badly stung, but from the lack of a decent killing agent on the market which I could consider as not only efficient, but capable of being safely stored around the house. I know that many anglers use mole fuses to destroy nests that are in the ground, pushing them into the entrance hole before digging them out and keeping them in covered containers till they are wanted – but the method has no appeal to me.

Once the decision was taken I watched the advertisement columns in a local paper and made contact with somebody who advertised himself as being a professional nest remover, and arranged to buy nests from him as he took them. Whatever their size, nests will need carefully dissecting if you want to get the most out of them. Remove the paper outer case to get at the grubs inside that are the hookbait. The best come from queen grubs that are big, plump and of a yellow colour, usually found at the top layer inside the nest itself. They are very delicate and need a fine wire hook if they are to be mounted without bursting open. Some anglers bake the nest to toughen the grubs – I prefer to use them as soon as possible in their natural state.

The remainder of the nest, including unwanted grubs and pupae, must be made into wasp cake. This can either by used as a hookbait or, with some additive, as groundbait. Powder everything in a large bowl until it is fine – dust fine if possible. That which is to be used for groundbait must have some extra-fine breadcrumb or one of the powder-type proprietary packet groundbaits added to provide weight and bulk. The complete mix can then have water added until it can be moulded into tight, small balls.

Where the cake is to be used as hookbait omit the crumb and scald the powdered cake with hot water, moulding it into small hook-sized balls while still warm. Each ball will cling and remain individual ready for use. Once prepared, both hookbait and groundbait are capable of being deep frozen until required.

Two or three balls of groundbait thrown into the head of a swim followed by two or three grubs mounted onto a size 8 or 10 hook and fished with a standard long-trotting rig can bring some spectacular sport, especially for chub, dace and roach. Mostly the float will slash sideways rather than give the traditional bob-type bite, an action probably caused by fish running through the swim then grabbing and swimming with the hook in one quick movement.

Wasp grub cake is a deadly bait when legered, not just during the summer months but in winter as well. Once on the hook it will tend to rise and float in the water, keeping it clear of the bottom. Pieces which break away either on the strike or during the cast will rise to the surface and fish will take them with enthusiasm.

In fact many anglers prefer to fish the cake as a surface bait, using a small weighted sub-controller to help cast and then to mark its position. Allow around 1.2m (4ft) between controller and baited size 8 hook and wait until the fish moves the controller before you strike.

Chapter 17

TAKING CONTROL

An occasion that took place back in the early 1960s, the introduction of the bubble float to angling, caused a near-riot. Like so many new items of tackle that have appeared it was immediately hailed as a fishing wonder, something which would guarantee the angler fish by the ton. Some of the hype stemmed from the fact that the bubble was constructed from what was then a reasonably new material, transparent plastic. Most of it centred around the fact that it opened up a whole new approach to fishing tactics. Both combined were sufficient to rocket it to the top of angling interest for several seasons.

But not all was joy and wonder. For game fishery owners and water bailiffs the new bubble float was nothing more than an updated and streamlined version of a poacher's tool, the otter board. In its crude form the otter was a piece of timber fastened to the reel line which supported several flies tied on long traces. Properly fished it allowed the flies to be manoeuvred into places that could not be reached by normal casting. Once the similarity was recognised then the bubble was immediately banned, anglers being threatened with prosecution if it was found to be in their possession let alone on the line or in the water. In fact stories circulated of anglers seen using one on Scottish waters having the float fired at by shotguns!

There was a vastly different report on the coarse-fishing front, however. There the carp-fishing explosion had taken place and the bubble float was hailed as a miracle that would allow light surface-baits to be cast over vast distances, or worked into selected places either with aid from the wind or the angler's line. But shrewd anglers were quick to spot some of the faults presented by the simple bubble.

On early models there was difficulty in getting water in and out through the single plug hole, a fault cured when two holes, one either side, were provided. Far worse was the difficulty experienced actually in seeing the float if a long cast had been made. A few anglers coloured the inside of the bubble to cure the fault – but that merely brought it back into the range of a normal float, visible to fish below the surface.

There were plenty of other disadvantages: the bubble gave little or no signs of a bite when it was used in rough water – and that included open stretches where wind raised waves. Weight that it gave to the line was fine for casting, but the

109

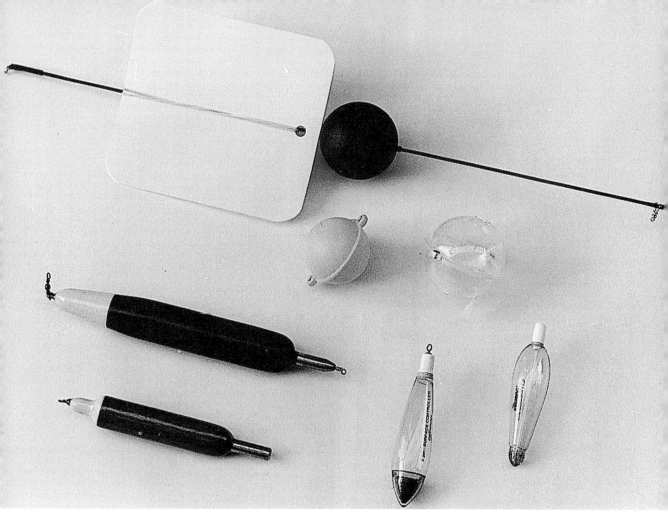

26. Top to bottom: the E.T. Drifter, both clear and coloured bubble floats, solid and transparent controllers and sub-controllers.

object of the exercise was quickly defeated when used on a small water or if it were badly cast towards an individual fish — the disturbance on landing immediately put every fish down.

Two other major problems presented themselves, the first connected with weedbeds. Where they were present it proved impossible for wind to drive or drag the float and its bait across them. Next, and far more important, was the fact that when a strike was made the float acted as a giant cushion, slowing the speed of the hook into the mouth of the fish.

But not all was doom and gloom. On shallow, still and clear waters where long-distance casting was unnecessary the float did bring results, especially on fisheries where fish were float shy. And when used underwater as a leger or paternoster weight to keep a bait in mid-water or free from the bottom then the action and results were first class.

So widespread use of the bubble float largely faded away for a time, but the need and requirements of carp fishermen for something which would control line either on the surface or underneath it when fishing large still waters remained. It was obvious that any replacement or improvement would need to be nearly or completely invisible, heavy enough to help cast a light bait over a long distance, and if necessary hold it in place once it was there regardless of the weather.

Today that problem is largely solved. Several controllers have appeared on the market that are designed to allow the angler a great deal of freedom when he uses floating baits. But automatically purchasing the first one that you see without thought is no guarantee to success, and some searching questions and honest answers must be asked and given before one is fastened to the line.

The first consideration should be whether the water to be fished is one that really demands the use of a controller. From my own observations on fisheries up and down the country I am sure that in a vast majority of cases the answer must be an emphatic no. Yet you repeatedly see small still-water carp fisheries where surface controllers are used in great sizes and cast with such energy that no self-respecting fish will put its head close to a surface-fished bait during the hours of daylight for fear of being knocked senseless.

It is always difficult to lay down hard and fast rules in fishing, but the criterion for using a surface controller must be that the water being fished should be so large that it would be impossible to reach distant areas where fish regularly patrol without the need for weight on the line. And even if the answer appears to suggest that that is the case, every possible means should be examined and tried to get the bait out without fastening a controller to the line.

In practice that means getting down to a water – not necessarily the one you intend to fish – and then concentrating on measuring just how far you can cast a floating bait using your normal tackle without losing it. Don't accept your longest cast as being your normal distance, it is the average distance that matters. Be prepared for a surprise and, more important, accept that no matter how good you might think your average may be it can be improved upon by experimenting with a longer rod, lighter line, or practice at swinging or releasing the bait. In time it may well be that you can reach that distant area without need of a controller at all.

Study the water where the bait will be fished, if need be with a pair of binoculars. Drag a weight across it and note whether there is any weed. If there is, then you must be prepared to make some desperately accurate casts to ensure that the bait will land in a clear area, besides using a controller large enough to carry across the beds without tangling when you retrieve line.

While you are dragging make a note of the depth of water and 'feel' the weight hitting the bottom so that you can gain some idea of its construction. If very deep the use of a sub-controller may well be ruled out, which could prevent a bait being anchored in place during rough weather. Knowing the construction of the bed will help you to gauge the size (weight) of sub-controller which will be needed to provide anchorage; heavy on gravel and lighter where there is mud that will discourage drag.

Remember the advantages and disadvantages of the surface controllers that are on sale. Those with a solid body are fine for areas where there is weed against which the sunken body will blend. Better for clear, open waters, especially those that are overfished, are the clear plastic models. Where controllers are attached by one end-ring it will pay to choose the biggest ring in relation to the size of controller. Line that doesn't run free or which jams when the bait is taken usually means a bait immediately rejected from the mouth of a fish.

Use the smallest controller that you can. Large ones cast over long distances produce disturbance – and disturbed fish take a time to recover and re-circulate on the surface. Plastic leger stops help to provide less resistance when a bite occurs and will allow the line to lie on the surface. A substitute lead shot used in its place will reduce free running of the line.

Sub-controllers are only as delicate and responsive as the amount of weight that anchors them to the bottom. Unnecessary weight will frighten fish, help to cause 'keyholing' (the action caused by the weight of the controller leading the bait during the cast, causing line to tangle with it) and where the bed has different foundations, i.e. mixed mud and gravel patches, drag the controller under water every time that the weight lands on a soft patch.

I prefer those models that allow line to be fed through the controller as opposed to line either led over a solid body, or tied to swivels at either end. Extra knots mean a reduction in line breaking strain and that in turn brings added and unnecessary risk.

Finally, the best controller cast to within a fraction of where a fish is or will eventually feed is wasted if the line between it and the bait does not float. Be prepared to examine and if necessary grease it before every cast.

One last controller – or rather float and controller combined – should be discussed although its use is confined to pike fishing. The need to work rather than cast a bait frequently occurs when you are piking on a still water. Sections of the bank which are overgrown with branches and brushwood hanging over the surface are no-go areas simply because a bait cannot be cast beneath them. A similar problem arises along stretches of the bank where dead reedmace stretches out into the water among whose stems and roots pike will lie sheltered and safe. To cast into them is tackle suicide. The only chance of success would be to work a bait up to and against the reed mass.

The E.T. Drifter is a cross between pike float and surface controller that uses wind to drag a bait where you want it to go. Its table tennis ball-sized body is pierced with a long, thin metal wire supporting a swivel at both ends through which reel line is passed. Above the body a large, square plastic sail can be fixed by the aid of rubber bands and depending on strength of wind combined with the direction from which it is blowing, plus sensitive work with the rod tip to control

27. *A common carp taken from the edge of a lake using a bubble float.*

the sail, either a floating or sunken bait can be propelled with comparative ease.

The Drifter has a further use. On vast areas such as the Norfolk Broads it can be launched and allowed to run and search for very long distances, presenting the bait without sight or sound from an angler. Used from a boat with the line well greased to keep it floating on the surface with little or no drag it is one of the most searching ways of pike fishing that I know.

One or two small snags that can occur with drift line fishing should be borne in mind. They are the greater the distance between controller and the bait, then the heavier will be the weight of line lying on the surface, which will in turn increase the resistance presented to the controller, no matter how fresh the wind may be. That means slower progress through the water – no great disadvantage for much of the time, but where there is extreme weather there can be a tendency for the sail to lie flat on the surface, bringing it back to the realms of being a normal float.

When a fish that is being played runs hard and deep below the surface it will

113

naturally drag the sail with it. In a surprising number of cases it will remain in place, especially if the rubber band which secures it to the body has been checked at regular intervals to make sure that it has not perished. Replacement sails are fairly cheap – but identical squares can easily be made at home, using thin plastic in a variety of colours to help show during bad light conditions so often experienced through the winter months.

Chapter 18

NEARLY NATURAL
ARTIFICIALS

I spend a considerable amount of my fishing time debating the word 'Why?' especially when it comes to assessing the value of artificial lures that are outside and beyond the normally accepted plug and spinner types. There has been a glut of them on the coarse-fishing market recently, many in the form of plastic, floppy and ugly imitation of a natural insect or invertebrate. Others look like a figment of the manufacturer's imagination, made to represent nothing to be found in freshwater.

They line the shop display stands in their bubble packs and plastic envelopes seemingly without a sale being made. Yet thousands of way-out lures do hit the water every week, though seemingly without arousing the slightest interest or comment from those who buy them. Which raises the big question again – why? Are they so good that everyone knows they are on to a good thing and keeps quiet about them? Or is it because they are completely and utterly useless and the angler is ashamed of being seen with them?

There is an entirely different attitude in game fishing. There the reservoir trout angler will take with him a box packed with lures many of which will represent little or nothing in the shape and form of a natural fly, insect or fish. Vivid colours, weird shapes – the trout man not only accepts them without question but also shows them to his friends, fishes with them, and most important of all catches fish. Which prompts the use of that word again – why?

Reason number one must be that the trout angler has complete confidence in his 'bait'. From long experience he knows that anything tied to the end of his line is a fur and feather fraud often offered to fish through frustration, when look-alikes that attempt to copy the natural have been tried and failed.

Reason number two is even more important. Anything that the trout man fishes with will be made to both look and act like something that is natural – if not credible – once it is in the water. Combine that with confidence and you begin to understand his reasons for success.

Hard though it is to admit, the coarse angler is schooled into using a bait that will work for him either by its own action once it is placed on the hook, or through its scent. Because of that he rarely bothers to look at an artificial bait, let alone getting round to thinking about how such a bait might be made to work. A sure-fire case of defeat purely through lack of imagination.

My interest in unconventional artificial lures goes back several years. In that time I have examined many, rejected some, regularly used a very few. In every case I have started by examining and studying the natural live item thoroughly before making a comparison with any artificial that may be on offer. Working in that way my study has occasionally led to a design of my own, or the alteration and adoption of an item already on the market. Here I shall describe half a dozen of them together with my reasons for their use or in some cases abandonment.

Studying the shallow area of a small lake one day where newts were surfacing at regular intervals to take in air, I was startled to see a fair-sized pike swing into the area and take one on its upward journey from the bottom. I had often considered that newts would be on the food list for many species of fish but had not really got around to doing anything about it. There were several reasons for this.

First of all there are several species of newt, all of which are protected in one form or another under regulations contained within the Wildlife and Countryside Act 1981. Specifically listed is the Great Crested Newt which at around 15cm (6in) long is the biggest of them all. At the other extreme is the Smooth Newt growing to 7–10cm (3–4in). Next came the fact that even if not protected it would take a fair amount of time to catch newts either with the aid of a worm tied to cotton or by netting them as they rose to the surface. Finally, and most important, I couldn't bring myself to mount something so prehistorically ugly – but attractive – on to a hook.

The alternative was to find or design an artificial of some sort. But it was some time before a solution presented itself and then only by accident. While sea fishing for bass off Beachy Head I was examining a Red Gill rubber sandeel. At that time I was experimenting with sandeels as a summer pike bait so decided to give one a try. It took a few good pike, and to my surprise two very good chub from below a small weir, one of which scaled 1.5kg (3lb 7oz).

What item of natural food did those fish 'imagine' a Red Gill represented? At 23cm (9in) long it hardly fell under the heading of leeches or other freshwater worms. The closest look-alike was the newt, though that was considerably smaller than the eel I was using. But the firm who make Red Gill baits produce a smaller lure some 6cm (2½in) long in both black and red colours. I quickly found these to be more killing than the large model.

To fish them use a fly rod with close-faced or fixed-spool reel holding line which is around the 1.3 kg (3lb) strength. Fix a lead substitute swan shot 0.6m (2ft) or so above the lure, cast as far as is possible parallel with and close to the bank from which you are fishing. Retrieve in a slow series of sink-and-draw actions making the lure rise and fall in the same way that the newt rises for air. Bites are immediate and mainly self-hooking.

Though newts mostly disappear from the water during late spring and early summer, not to return until the following season, the artificial look-alike will continue to score throughout the year. I prefer the larger Red Gill during winter used with a soft wire trace to prevent bite-offs from pike.

Close to the newt in swimming action is the elver. Great shoals of them run our rivers in spring when they are 5–7cm (2–3in) long and fish of every sort go mad for them. I have caught chub using an elver head-hooked and float fished which, once on the bank, disgorged several elvers which they had taken before mine but had not swallowed them. But there is a drawback with fishing elvers; they are available for a short period only, even though they remain attractive to fish long after they have spread upstream and dispersed.

It is possible to freeze them, wrapping them individually after being thoroughly washed and dried. I found that when water conditions were right for their use I had invariably left them at home. The answer was to use an acceptable artificial that could be carried at all times and again, I found one by accident.

An article in the American *Field and Stream* magazine from the 1960s showed and described the Serpent Fly, 'a bug-eyed, fuzzy-bodied long-tailed creation made to tantalize the most reluctant winter bass'. Studying it I realised that whatever it was made to represent in the States, it was a dead ringer for elvers in this country.

Peter Dean, the Professional Fly-tier who lives in Eastbourne, tied some for me using black and drab brown hackles with extra-long saddle hackles to provide that vital snakelike motion when they were retrieved. The big eyes fastened to the head certainly impressed me, if not the fish, while a little lead substitute wrapped around the shank of a size 6 hook provided sufficient weight to make the lure slowly sink.

Fished slowly, using a long rod which is necessary to provide control over the lure, plus a fine line with a little substitute lead fastened 0.45m (18in) or so above the hook this imitation elver has given me chub, perch, pike, carp and trout in both still and running water throughout the warm months, which in our greenhouse-heated world extends through to early November.

It was Peter Dean who gave me another perfect imitator. Sitting in his bungalow, watching ducks on his decoy pond and discussing artificial lures in general he suddenly asked whether I had tried the imitation tadpole. I admitted that I knew there was a fly of that name but had not tried it. Peter then introduced me to the Mad Tom.

The originator of this pattern was an American, and when Peter first heard of it he tied and tried some on large lake trout at a nearby fishery. The day was warm, it was early spring and Peter had no success with the trout whatsoever. He did, however, connect with some hefty carp, besides hooking and losing several others. Mystified as to why carp should be interested in such an uninspiring lure Peter watched the water and realised that it was alive with great shoals of half-

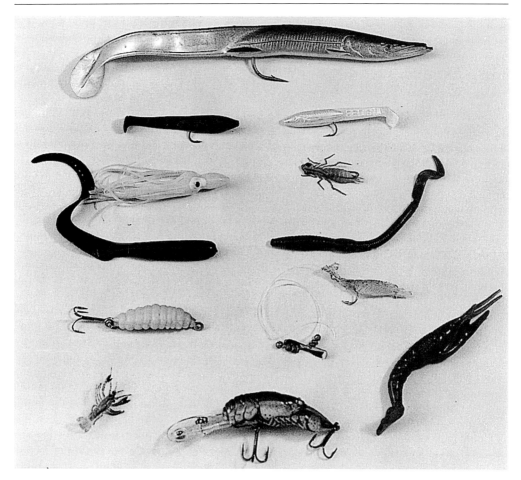

28. Top to bottom: Redgills, both large and small, plastic squid and nymph, American-style plastic worms, plastic crayfish and the Rebel Crawfish.

grown tadpoles and that the carp were running riot through them.

He gave me a selection of the black hackled, twin tail lures tied on size 10 to 6 hooks. Cast with the aid of a fly rod and the line gently stripped back to you in 15cm (6in) pulls, it will allow this king-sized taddy to bumble along just under the surface like the natural it so neatly imitates. It has given me roach, chub, trout, and carp through the summer months and I wouldn't be without it. They are also very successful dapping lures, the spread of hackles making firm dimples across the surface of the water.

In a previous chapter I have written on the success of crayfish as a bait, together with suggestions for a natural alternative. Our cousins across the Atlantic have a crustacean that looks very similar to ours which they call the crawfish, equally attractive as a fishing bait. Americans demand a more sporting

29. *Top to bottom: two jigs, below them two poppers. Two Serpent flies and a Mad Tom complete the picture.*

outlook to fishing than we do, and I was not surprised to discover that the Rebel Bait Company listed a crawfish (crayfish) look-alike plug in their catalogue. Surprised at finding anything in the plug world made to imitate anything that is natural, I immediately sent for one.

At 8.5cm (3½in) long this floating/deep diver looks every inch the same as our English crayfish. Accurate moulding of the tail segments and separate 'claws' make for attraction, treble hooks being mounted under the abdomen and at the end of the claws. The deep diving vane is mounted at the tail which means that the lure is retrieved backwards – the same way in which a crayfish moves in real life.

Cast under banks and close to weedbeds, then worked in a succession of short and rapid retrieves from the reel this plug can be made to imitate the real thing like no other plug I have fished with. In still or running water I have rarely left the banks without accounting for chub, perch and pike. Battered and worn, with the eyes practically missing, my last copy is still as killing as the day it was first used. And in the company of many anglers reduced to a single copy of an old favourite, I am now loath to use it for fear of losing it.

Included in the photograph of the Rebel Crawfish (photograph 28) are several plastic imitation crawfish which were on offer for some time in this country. The largest is a soft, limp casting designed to be mounted on a hook rig of your own choice and presumably (instructions were not attached) designed to be fished in the same way as a plug. I had no success with it, despite a very fair trial. Nor did I have any with the tiny Burke Fishing Lure Company's Flyrod Crawfish.

Other plastic lures that are illustrated have also proved to be fruitless for me, despite the fact that the imitation dragonfly larva is a pretty faithful representation of the live insect. I feel that the reason for failure with these copies lies in the fact that they cannot be made to imitate the movements of the live counterpart in the water.

Possibly weight has something to do with it; definitely flexibility or the lack of it must play a part in rejection. Even the plastic worm, beloved of American fishermen, has failed me despite long and thorough trials in a variety of waters. Yet in smaller sizes there is a remarkable resemblance of the worm to our leeches.

At the other extreme are poppers, small wooden-bodies lures with floppy rubber legs and feathered tails that float, and with the aid of a scoop-shaped head can be pulled, or 'popped', across the surface of the water. They look like nothing on earth, yet fish extremely well. Dapped on the surface between high bankside bushes or cast and worked under trees with the aid of a long rod, I can only imagine that they must be accepted by fish as insects that fall into the water. On stretches where chub shoal and there is an 'eat first, wonder what it was after' type of competition for food they do exceptionally well.

One final lure, again from the States, that bears thought and demands use is the jig. A large metal head cast onto a big single hook, dressed with gaudy feathers that cover bend, point and shank of the hook itself completes the jig. Some variations to the dressing allow for the use of glitter strip, other variations are to the colour of the large eye painted on each side of the head.

The loop for attaching line is above the head, which means that however the jig is retrieved the head will always keep on an even keel. By virtue of its weight (up to 28g/1oz is normal) it can be cast for considerable distances and then worked back in a succession of sink-and-draw actions. Better still is to fish the jig from a boat into deep water, where it can be 'bounced' across the bottom.

I have done exceptionally well using jigs in large weirpools, especially on the River Thames where their weight allows you control and to keep in touch with the lure through the line no matter how rough the water may be. In particular they are excellent for big, cannibal Thames trout — even when feathers and dressing are nearly rubbed from the body through work.

Chapter 19

WORKING ON THE SURFACE

Nobody could accuse Izaak Walton of having angling hang-ups. When he and his trusty 'A' team were doing their rape and pillage act up and down the River Lee, usurping milkmaids as well as nobbling all open sweepstakes, their catches there were fish in plenty for the angler. One has only to read his description of finding a hole where 'a dozen or twenty chevins would float near to the top of the water' to get some idea of the good life as it was. Undoubtedly he would settle for a coronary and early retirement if he could see those same place today, drained nearly dry by a Water Authority.

But not everything was bent rod tips and wet landing nets for those old boys. There were some problems along the river banks, the biggest and most difficult featured in the pages of the *Complete Angler* as big fish which always appeared to be staked out in unapproachable positions. Weed growth, both in the water and along the banks, was described as the 'root' cause, which prevented the angler from casting his horsehair-tied hook over a fish. Undoubtedly it was this single problem that led old Izaak to invent (or should that be publicise?) the noble art of dapping.

Dapping is a great sport and as much a line stretcher in today's angling world as it has been in the past. In fact today's hot summers and lack of water provide the perfect background to help with its success rate. It involves dropping a baited hook through seemingly impossible bankside vegetation to rest (dapp) on the surface of the water where it can be seen by a fish. In the past there has been some corny stuff written about the style, much of it straight from the pages of the *Complete Angler* and accepted as gospel.

There has also been great play made of anglers creeping along the bank, their rods rigged with barleycorn leads mounted above the hook to draw off line, or line wrapped around the rod tip so it could be unwound gently to lower the hook onto the water. All good stuff, but remember that old saying 'by method and rule lived many a fool'.

Start by mentally imagining when you could, or should, dapp. If you follow tradition it will only be when the sun is in the heavens, fish can be seen, with summer at its radiant best and insects at their height of abundance. Rubbish! That, in theory at least, is when you could expect the maximum return for your effort. But in practice you don't need to see fish to entice them by dapping; the season of the year is irrelevant, sun is not important and there only needs to be one insect on the water – yours.

What is important is that you know the water be it still (yes, you can dapp equally well on lakes or ponds) or a stretch of a river or stream. You will need to know the banks as well as you do the bottom and that includes every bush or tree of any consequence. More important still is the need to know exactly where fish lie at any given moment.

Armed with that information you are on the way to success. Knowing the few (and glaringly obvious) occasions when you should not dapp will ensure you get complete success. None of it requires concentration, just common sense.

Dapping is 90 per cent a visual style of angling. Fish that circulate in the vicinity of the surface always have an eye to the main chance and should something appear on or close to it they will respond by inspection and acceptance. Frequently there is little or no time between the two happenings. But there are some subtle overtones that can be brought into play when light levels are low, visibility is bad, and fish to all intents and purposes are 'blind'.

These centre around vibration. We have already discussed the fact that fish are conditioned to this, responding to the splash of groundbait, hempseed and so on as they land on the water. The same theory applies when a dapped bait is dropped deliberately on the surface, or worked up and down on it to produce good vibrations. Though not seen, it is automatically grabbed.

This is not an uncommon occurrence. In fact I am sure that there are not many anglers who have not had something similar happen when a fish whose presence they were unaware of suddenly made a grab at a float or plug the moment that it landed on the surface. But there are limits. Water that looks as though it has escaped from the local curry house must restrict the chances of a bait receiving attention, despite the appeal of vibration. And flood water that usually accompanies such colouring naturally stops the hook from remaining on the surface long enough to get attention of any sort. But flood water is about the only stop to the style.

Size, i.e. area of water, most definitely isn't. In fact the biggest mistake would-be dappers make is assuming that a water is too big, or that it is too small. They assume that any old rod will do, as will the line and hook. They assume that any old bait or fly will take a fish. And above all, they assume that just by keeping quiet and out of sight, every fish in the water will be fooled into being hooked.

Sheer boloney! Let's look first at the question of using the right tackle, starting with the rod. Yes, any old one will do – but try manoeuvring 4.2m (14ft) of delicate carbon fibre through trees and bushes alongside a tiny stream and see how you cope. Of course, the books will tell you that the long rod will enable you to keep back, out of sight, and fish 'fine and far off'. What they don't tell you is that while you are set 2.4m (8ft) back from the water you won't be able to see what's happening on the surface – and that's where the action will occur.

The ideal rod is one that will allow you vision *and* control so it must vary with the size of water that you fish. It must be said again, with emphasis, that if the matchman can frequently change his tackle during a day's fishing to suit the water, then so must the freelance angler who practises many different styles.

Present-day monofiliment is soft, camouflaged and largely without glint. But don't believe all that the manufacturers tell you; despite treatment the best of lines can reflect the sun. Better be sure than sorry — try the line first before embarking on some specimen hunting. Using a line of suitable strength is also important. Too great a diameter renders it visible, too small and fish will break free. And if the line is out of balance with the rod then there will be little chance of getting it to run through the rings and down to the water without a great deal of trouble.

Fixed-spool reels can be clumsy when it comes to releasing small amounts of line without resorting to savage jerks and snatches, especially when you are poking a rod through bushes or tall reedmace. I stick to a closed-face model where loose line cannot sag between pick-up and first ring, or use a good, old-fashioned centre pin.

Baits? Again, largely common sense. Given a wet or windy day when line is likely to cling to the rod or get twisted around rings I plump for a king-sized slug,

30. The Crane-fly, or daddy longlegs. Dapped and worked across the surface it is irresistible to chub.

one of those that look capable of mugging an elderly lady gardener. Its weight will carry both hook and line easily to the water without resorting to lead on the line or physical jerks.

But the beauty of dapping lies in the small amount of gear you need to carry around to practise it. Bait boxes are a pain – and planned baiting unnecessary. If natural baits are needed then grasshoppers, caterpillars, bugs, moths and other creepies can generally be found along the banks. Far better to use an artificial lure, backed by a lead substitute swan shot pinched 15cm (6in) or so above the hook for weight.

You don't need to be a connoisseur to select an artificial fly. Crane-flies (daddy longlegs) happen to be my favourite and they can be brought ready tied at the tackle shop. But if the truth be told any other of the legion of reservoir trout lures that are available, regardless of their gaudy colours and overpowering size, will bring success. With dapping it's not so much what it is, but how you do it.

All of which leads directly to presentation. I've found a dividing line which splits that thorny problem into high and low bank approaches. Low banks are the easiest, allowing you to creep on hands and knees without showing above bankside herbage that might be growing. By comparison high banks are the very devil to fish from; the moment you make a direct approach you are over the skyline and you will be seen. The only possible solution is to make a sideways approach down on the water's edge, and that can be more than difficult, especially when balancing rod and net on a steep slope.

There is a great deal to be said for preparation when difficult banks of any sort must be fished. Where it is possible, and the size of fish that might be hooked worth the effort, then try erecting a hide and leaving it in place for 24 hours or so before you fish. It need not be elaborate – a camouflaged net from a Government surplus store costs little. Even a piece of black plastic fixed between two sticks cut from a hedge can suffice. It's a simple matter to creep up behind it and fish from over the top or round the sides without being spotted. Likewise plan a little for the steep and high bank by making a path through any scrub that lies along the base, and cutting footholds into the earth so that you don't slip and slide.

Most anglers interpret the word dapping to mean bobbing the bait up and down so that it just touches the surface of the water. In its pure form that is correct – but letting it sink just below the surface and then drawing it back up again is equally attractive and positively killing. It can especially be recommended when fishing 'on spec', without sight of a fish to cast over.

So also is swinging the bait out towards mid-water, letting it land and then gently and slowly dragging it back to leave a small surface wake during the retrieve. I've had this approach score handsomely during mid-summer, when the theorists would have us believe that surface drag in any form will put fish down before they take the hook. In fact some of my biggest rudd have been taken by this simple action.

Last, but by no means least, do have a place in mind where the hooked fish can be landed. This means planning in advance, something the majority seem loath to do. Perhaps it is connected with the 'bad luck to anticipate' syndrome so popular with anglers of all ages.

And remember it is not just chub that will be taken when you dapp. Whichever style you use can bring tench, carp, roach and rudd. I've even had an eel swipe at and take a large lobworm, and when that happens to you late in the evening you can take it from me that a whole new vocabularly of angling words are born that old Izaak would never have dreamed of.

INDEX